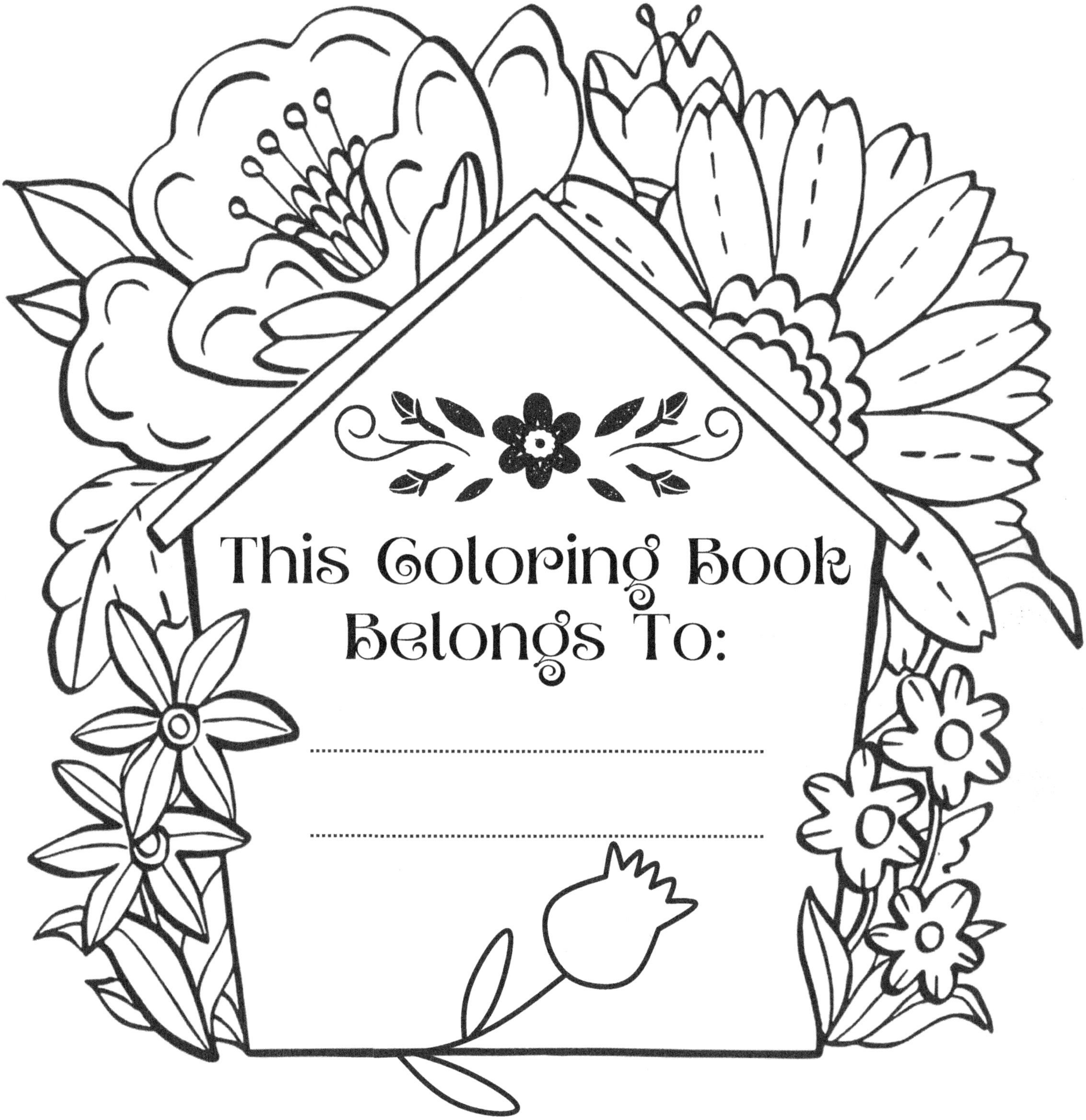
This Coloring Book
Belongs To:

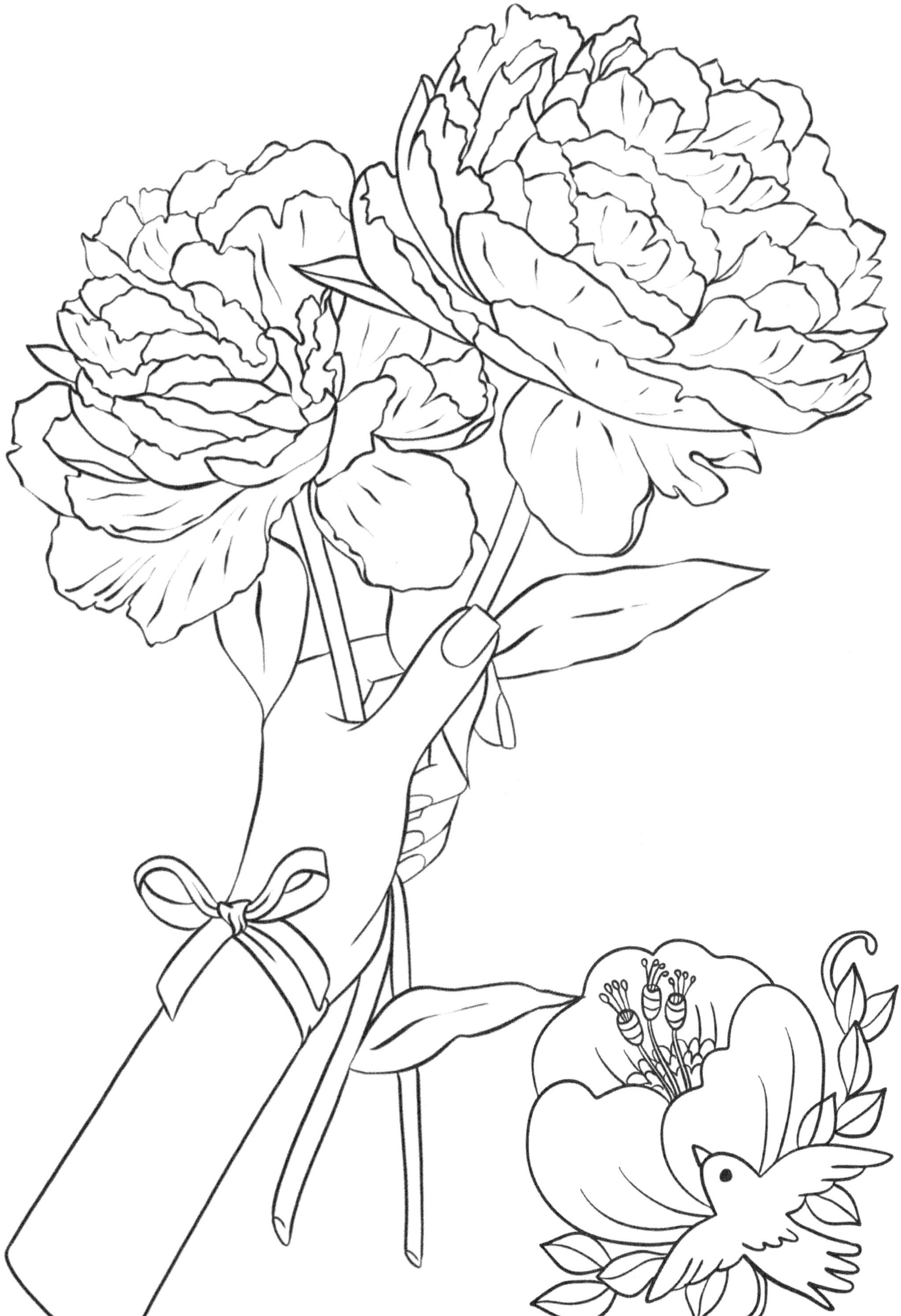

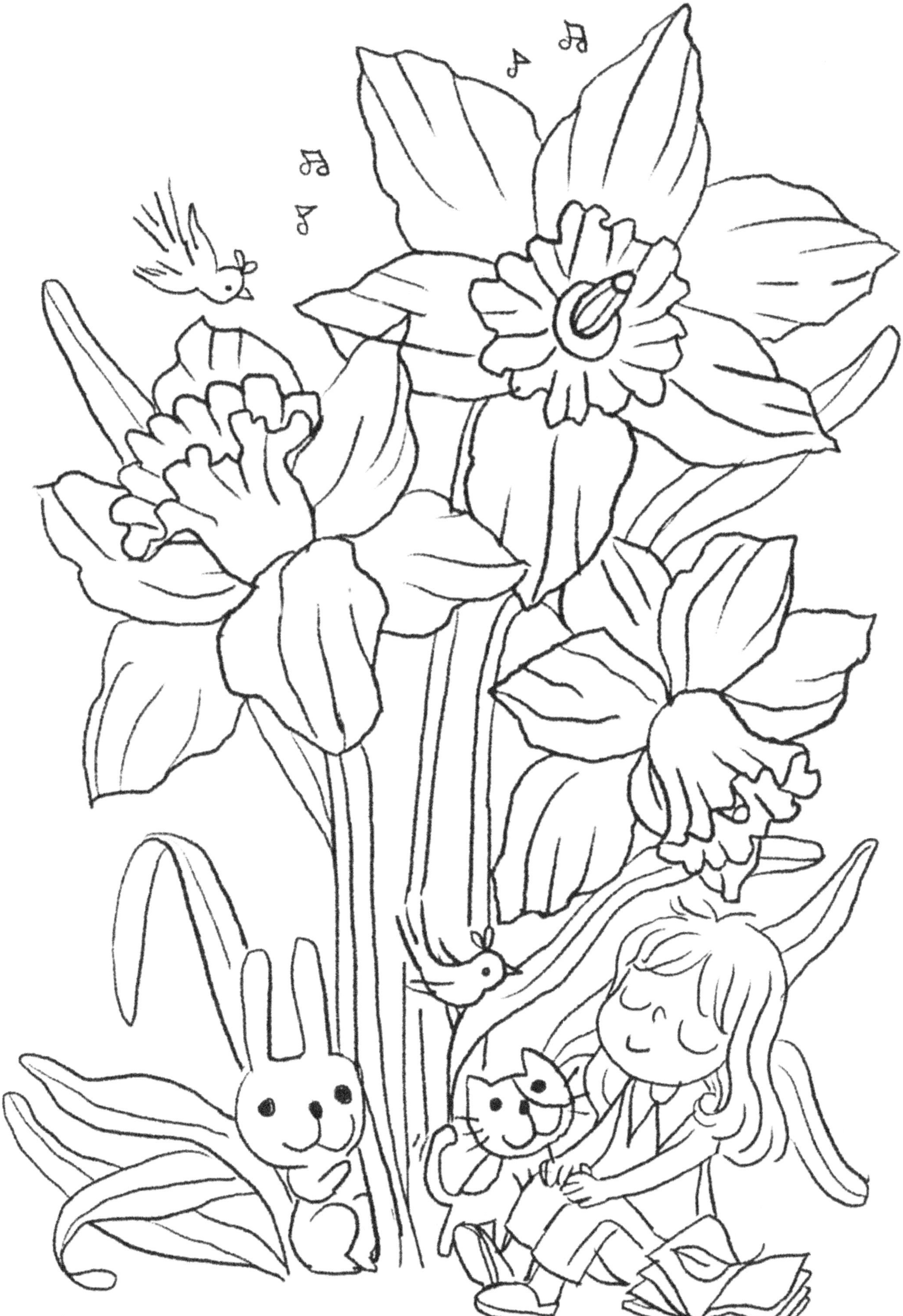

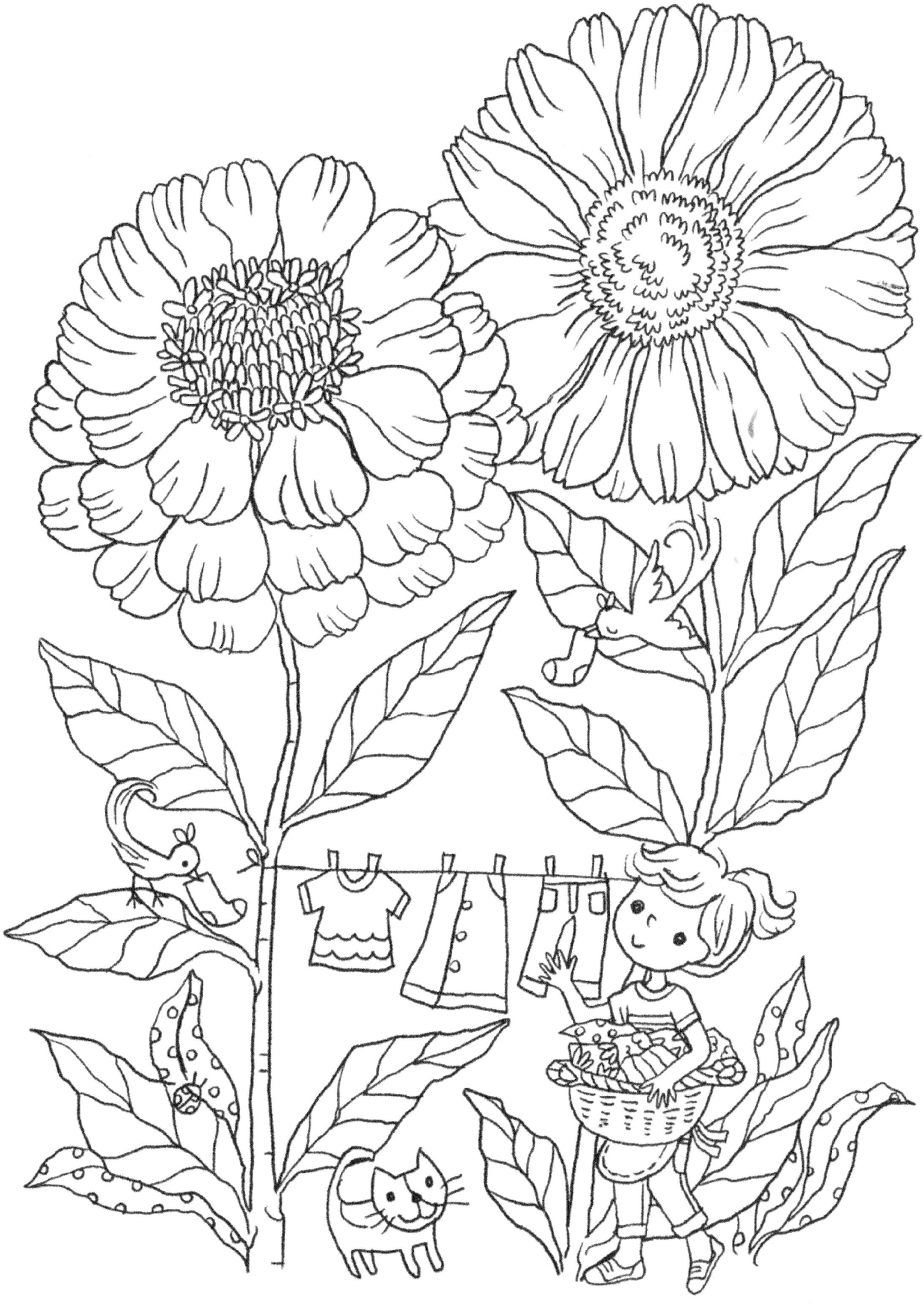

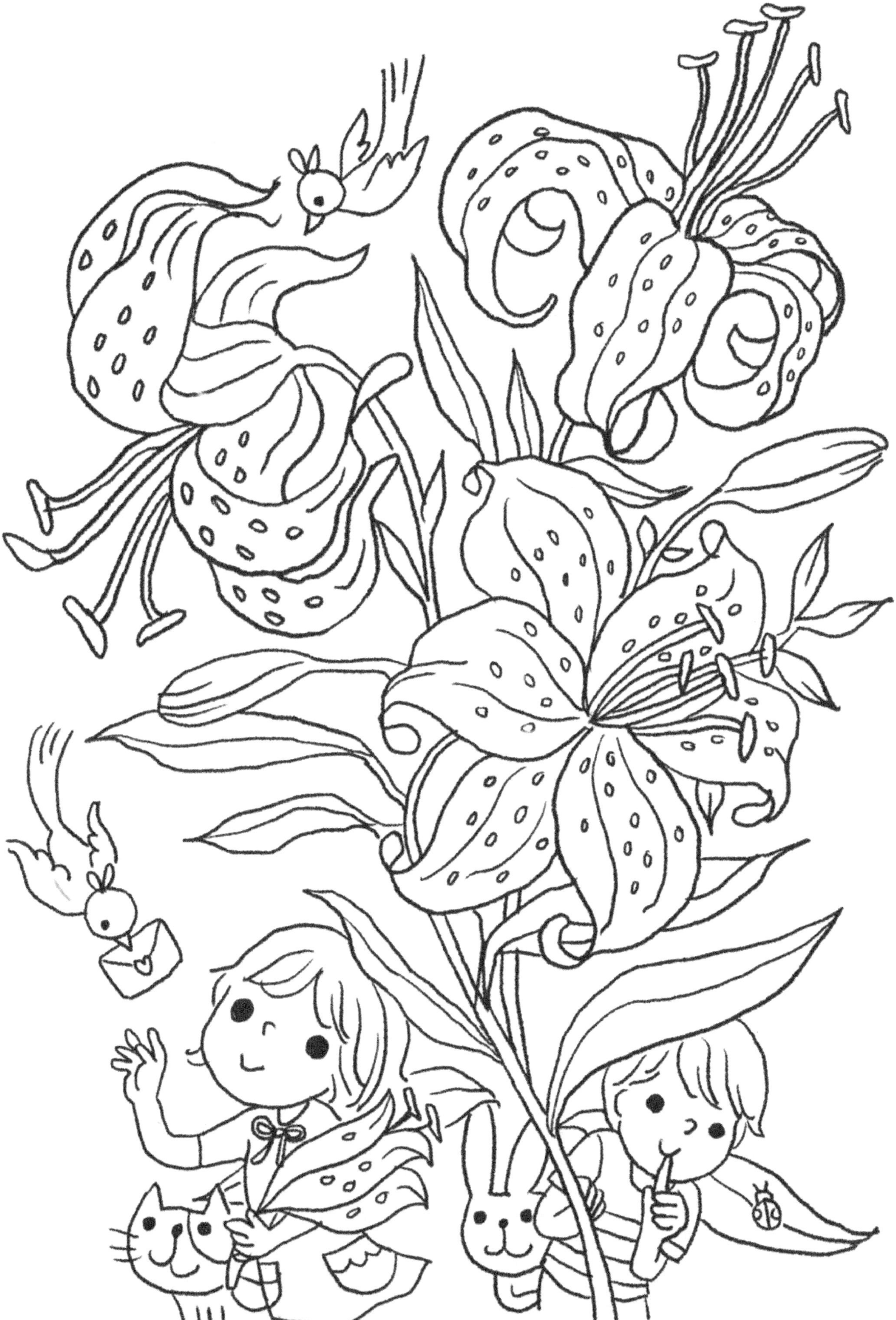

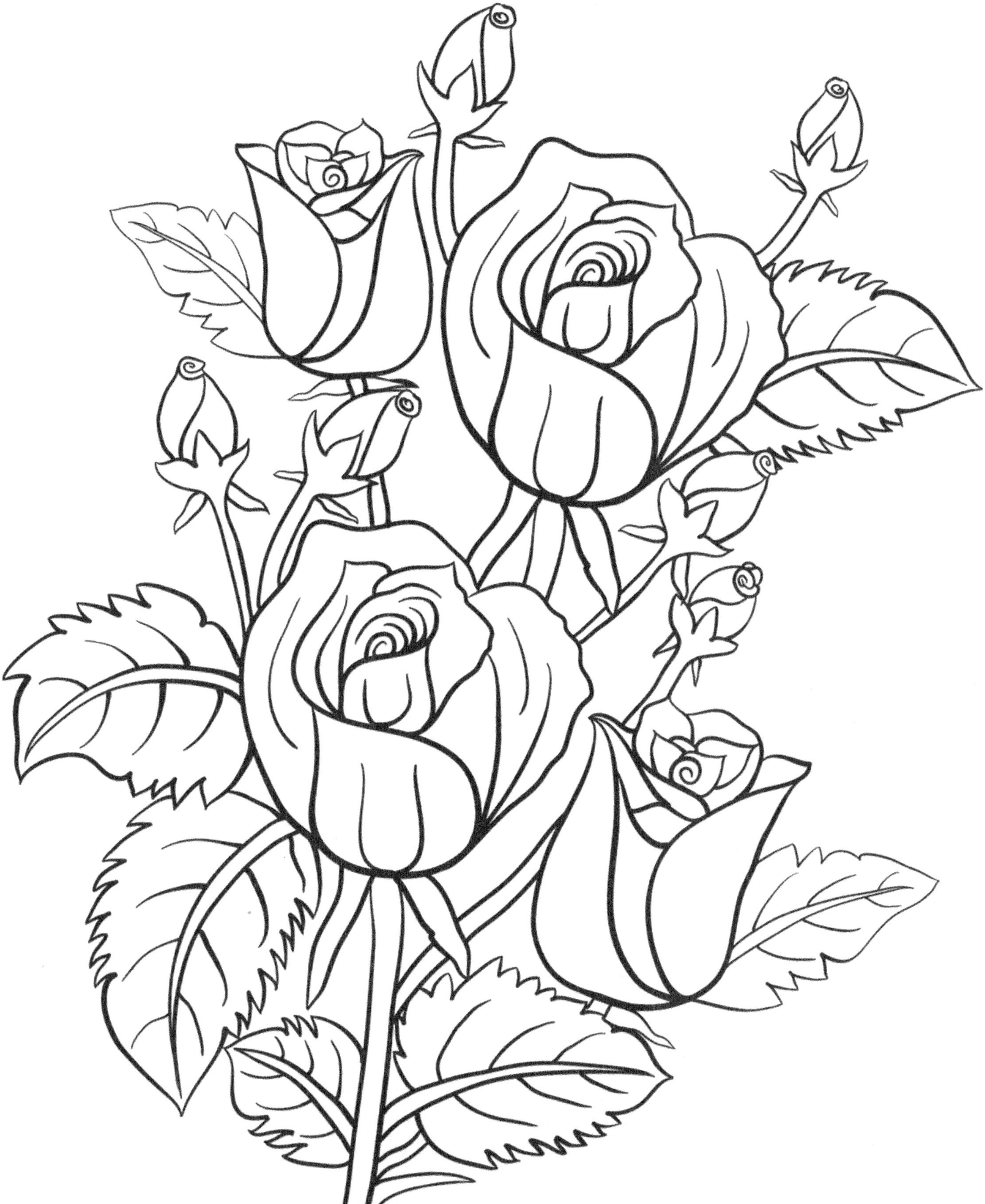

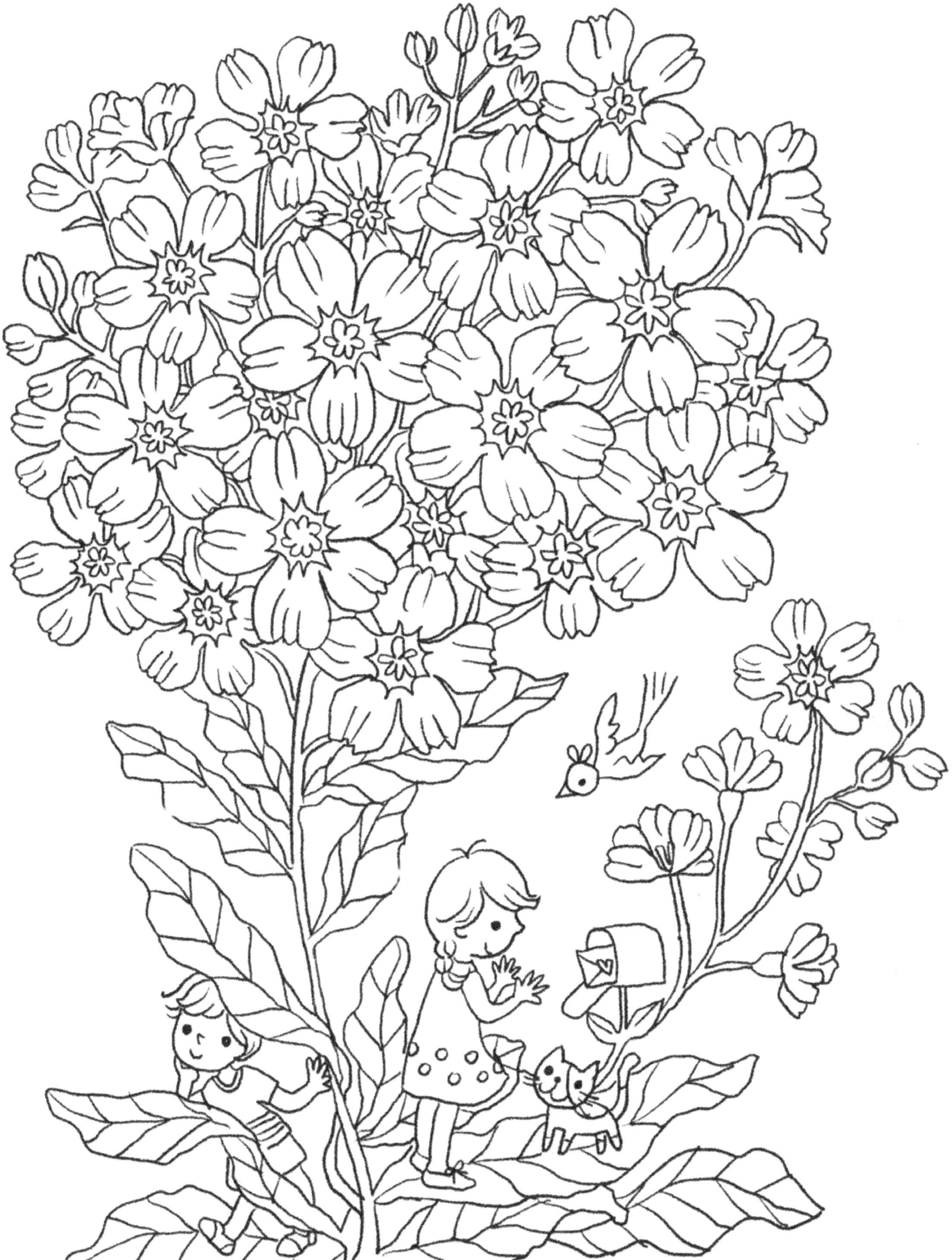

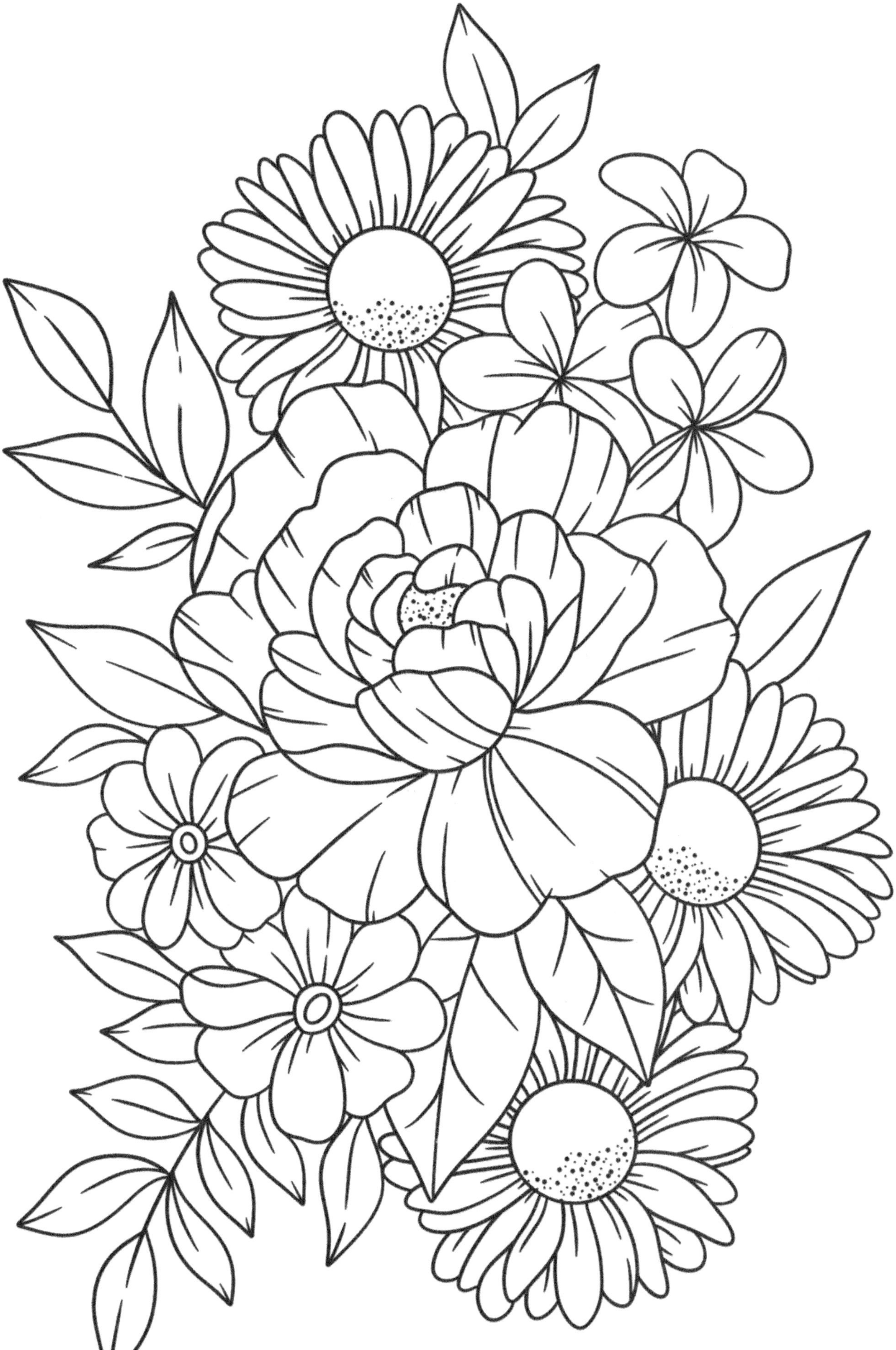

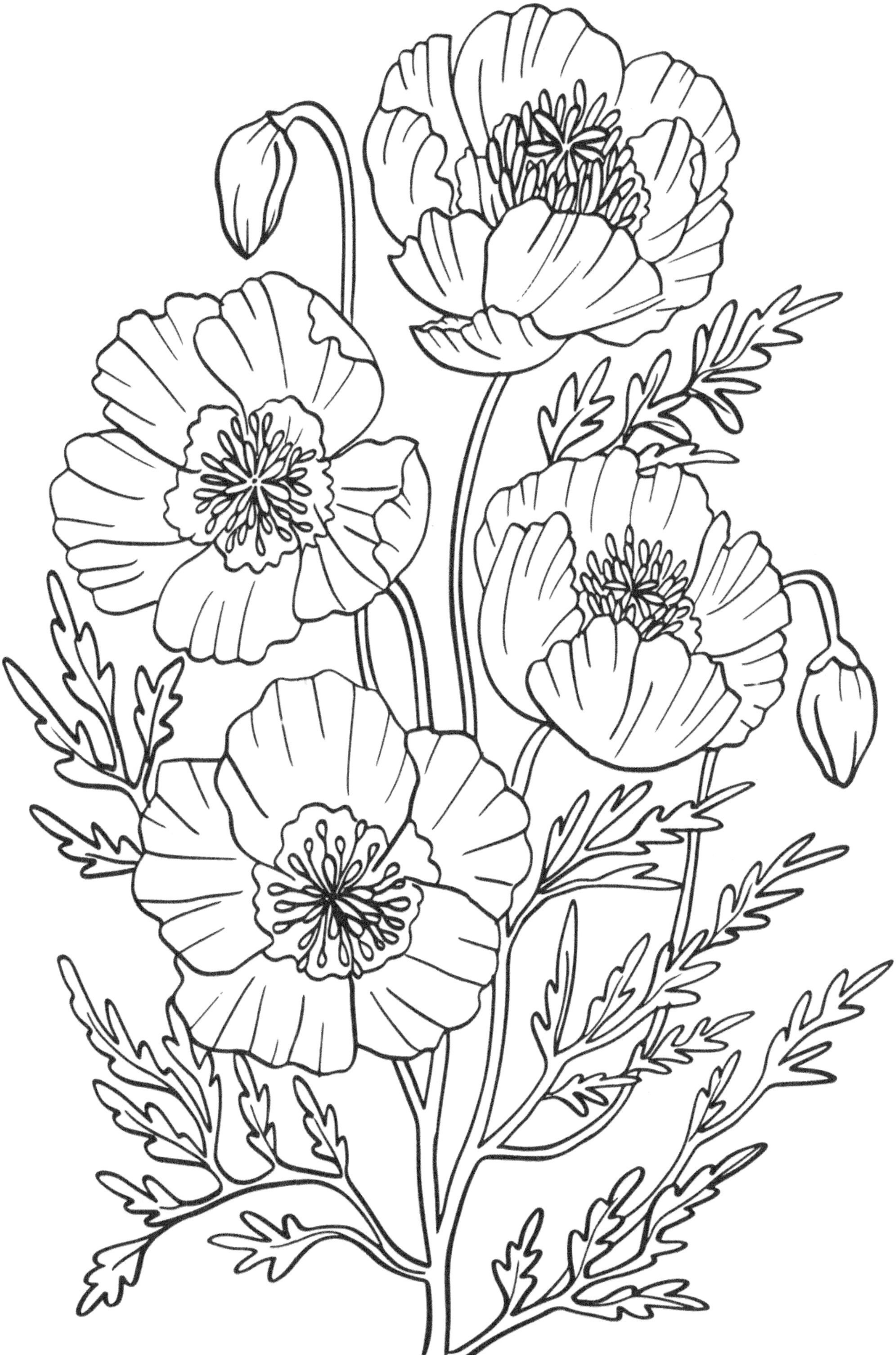

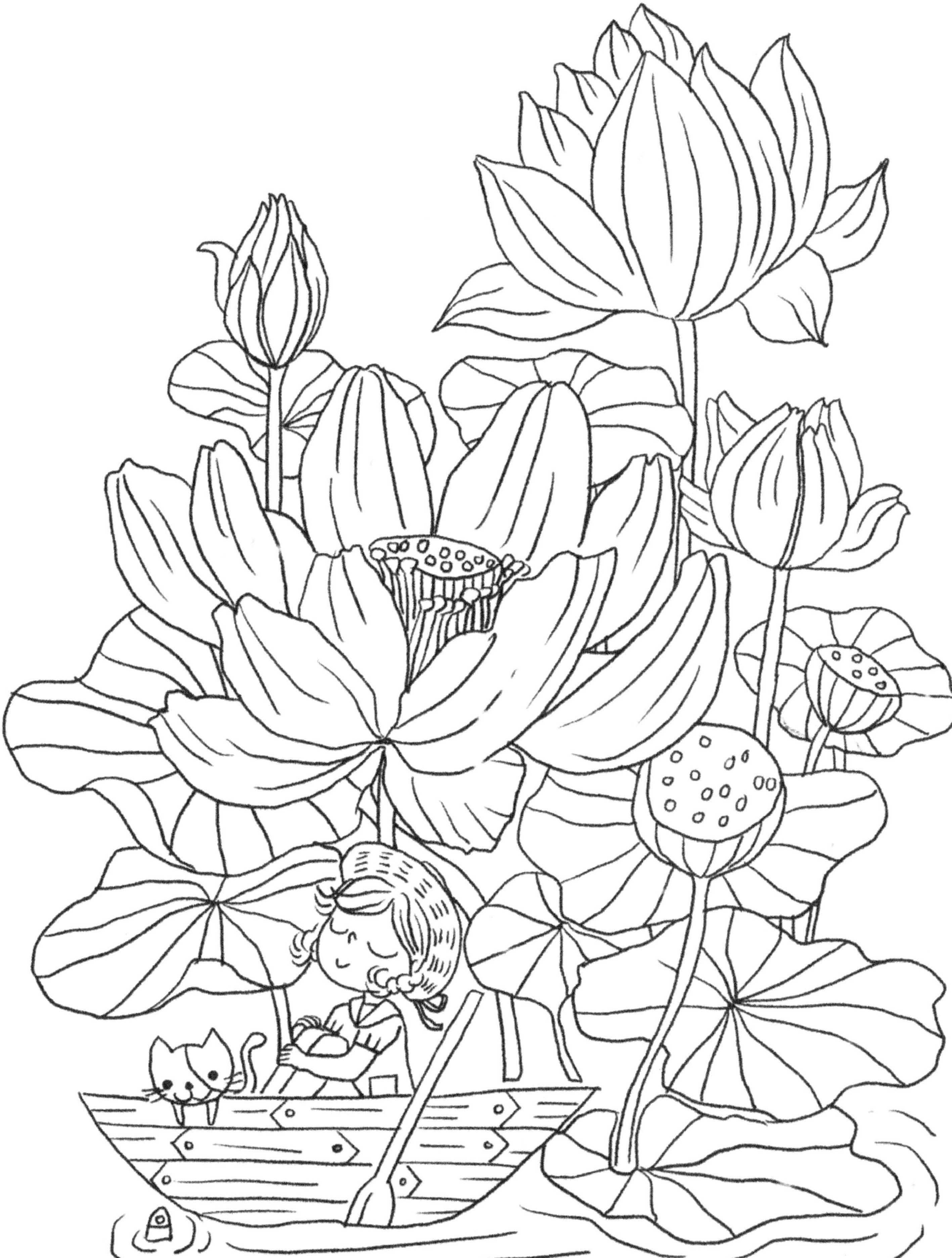

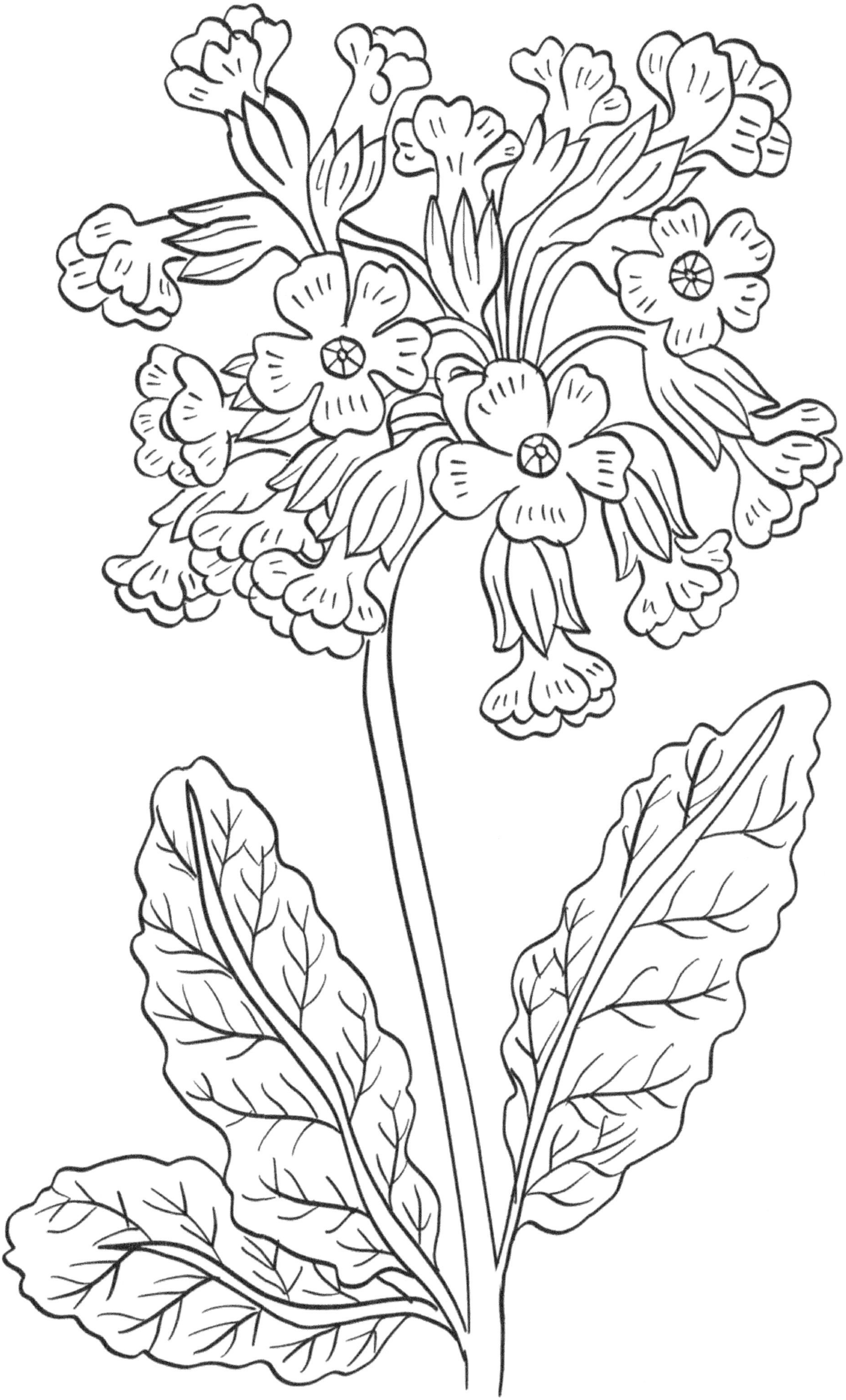

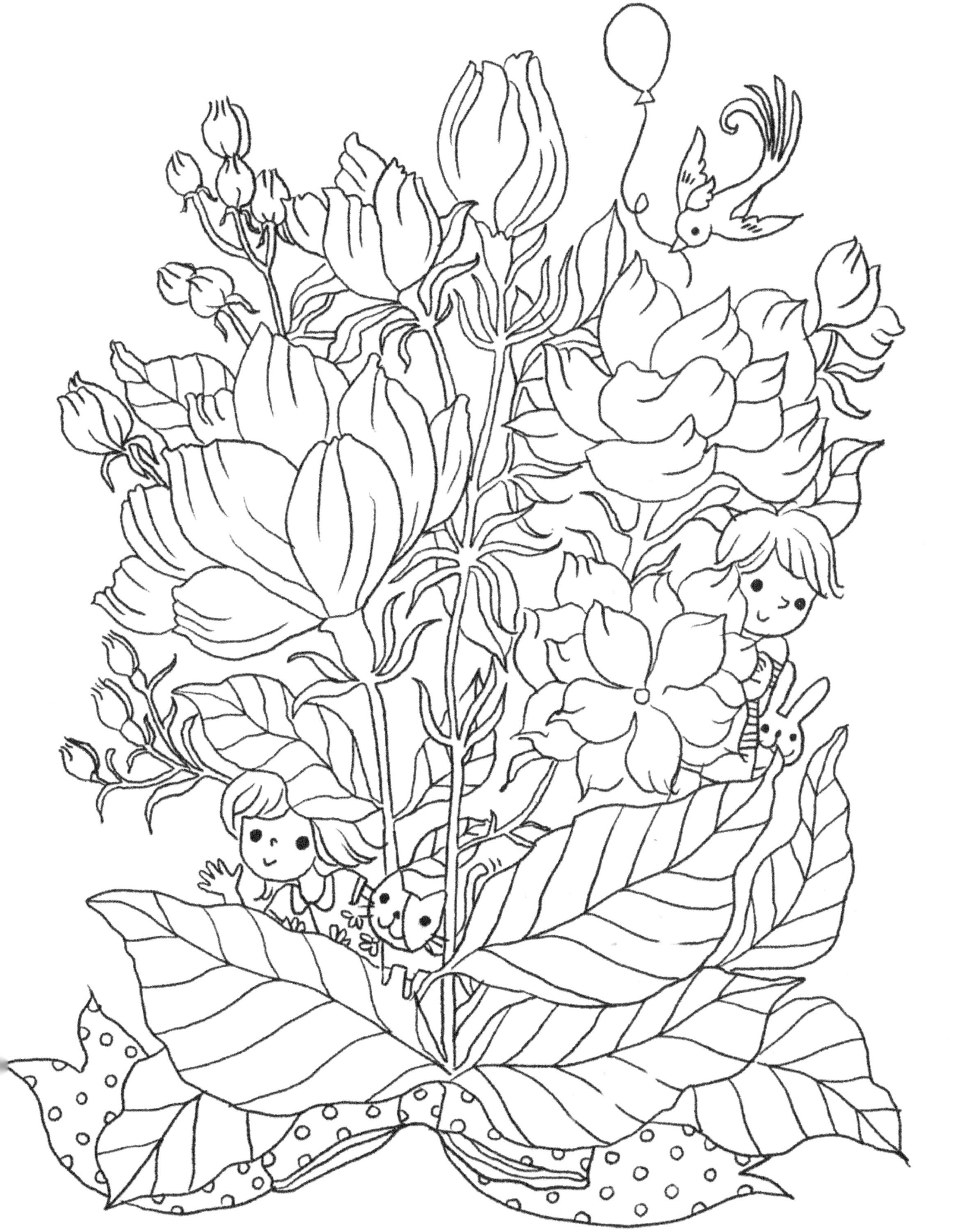

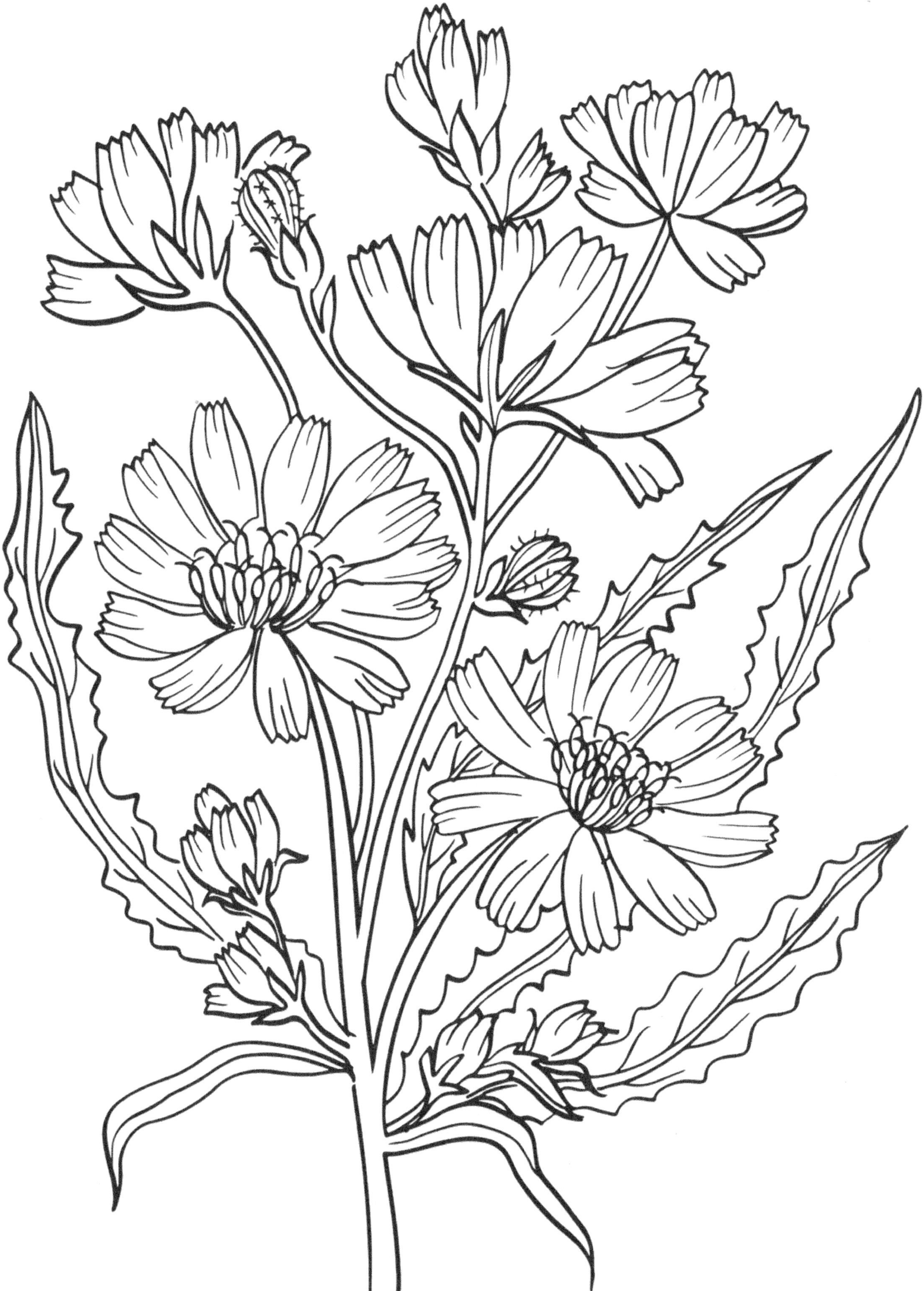

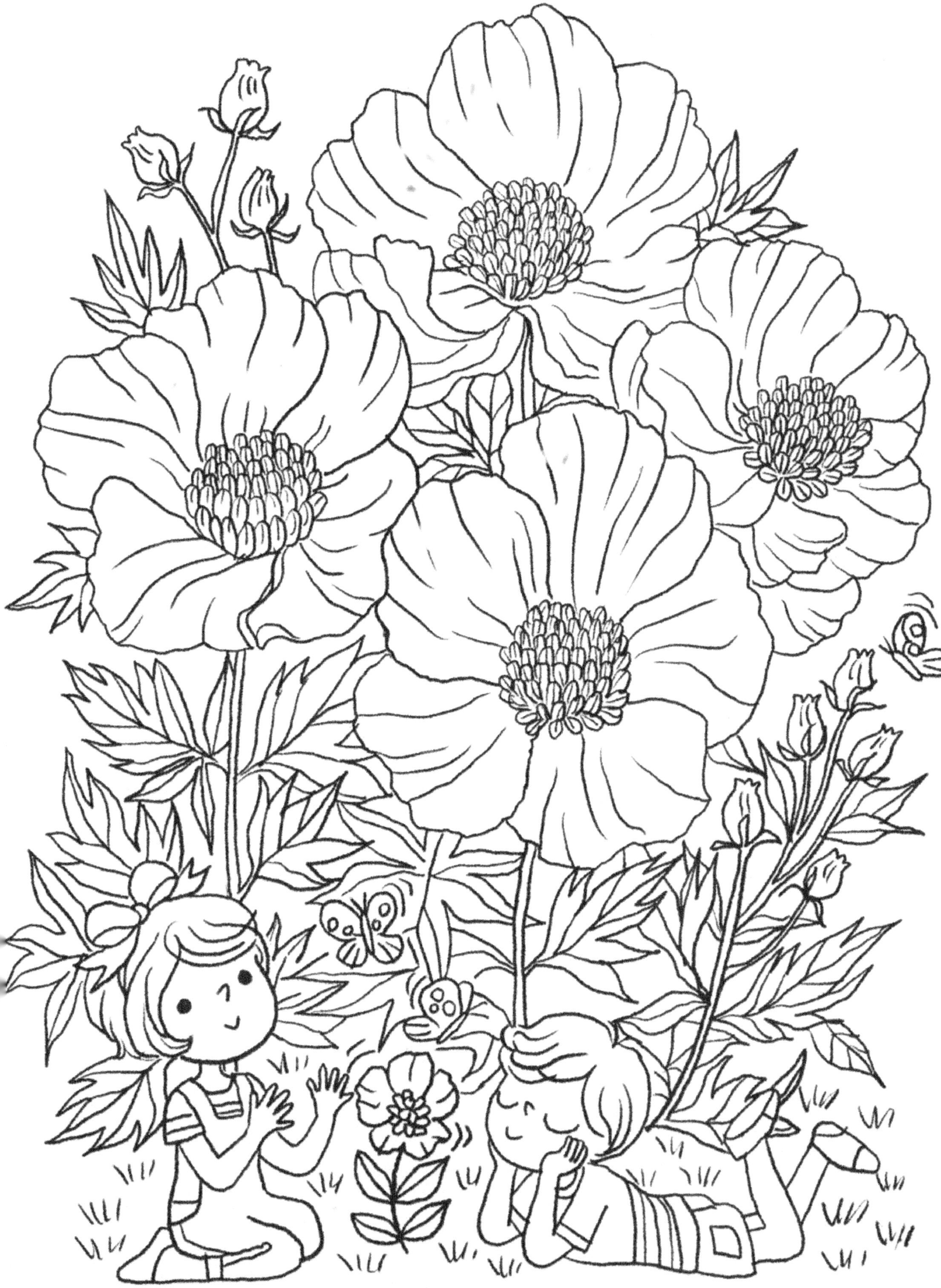

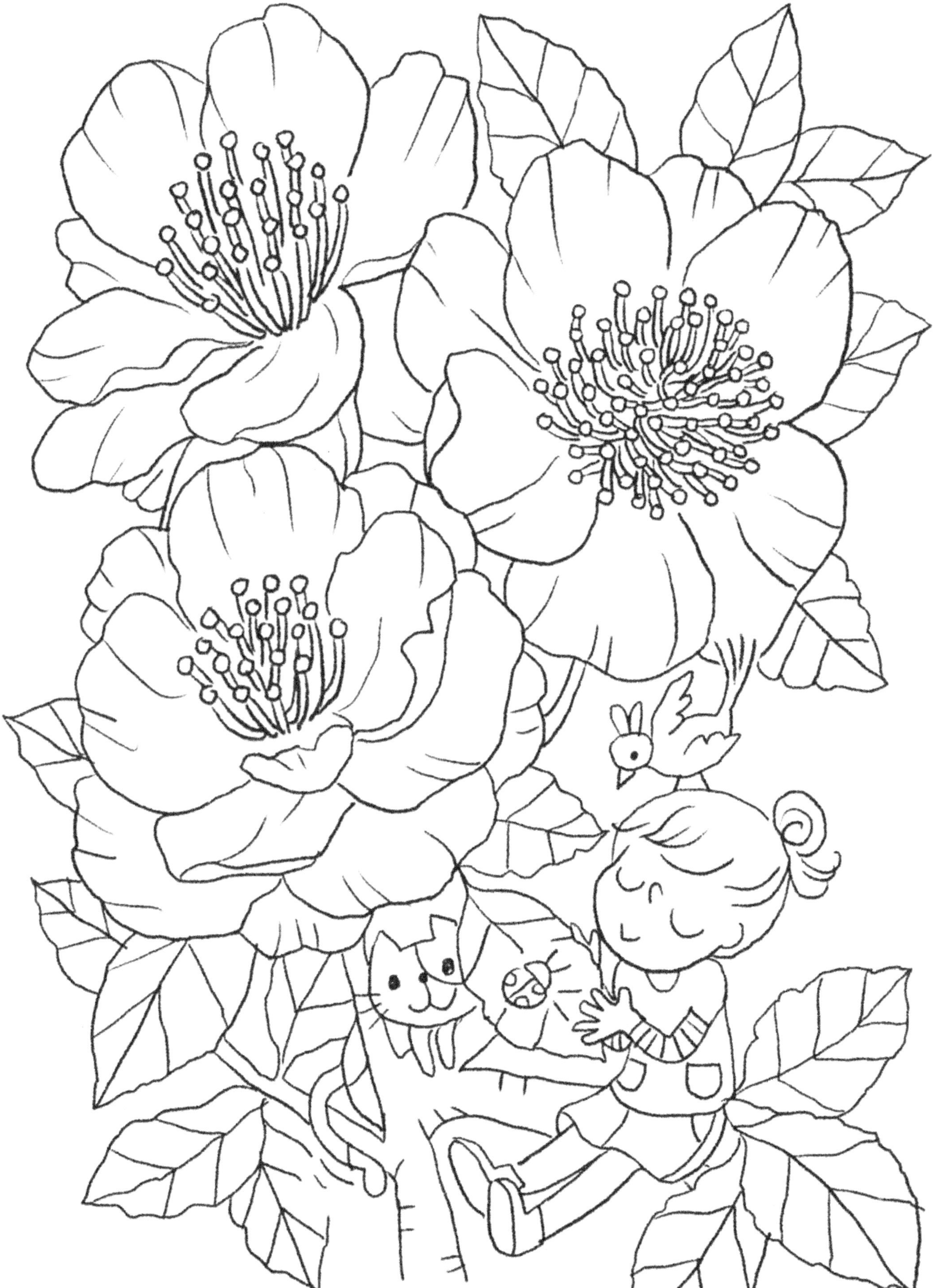

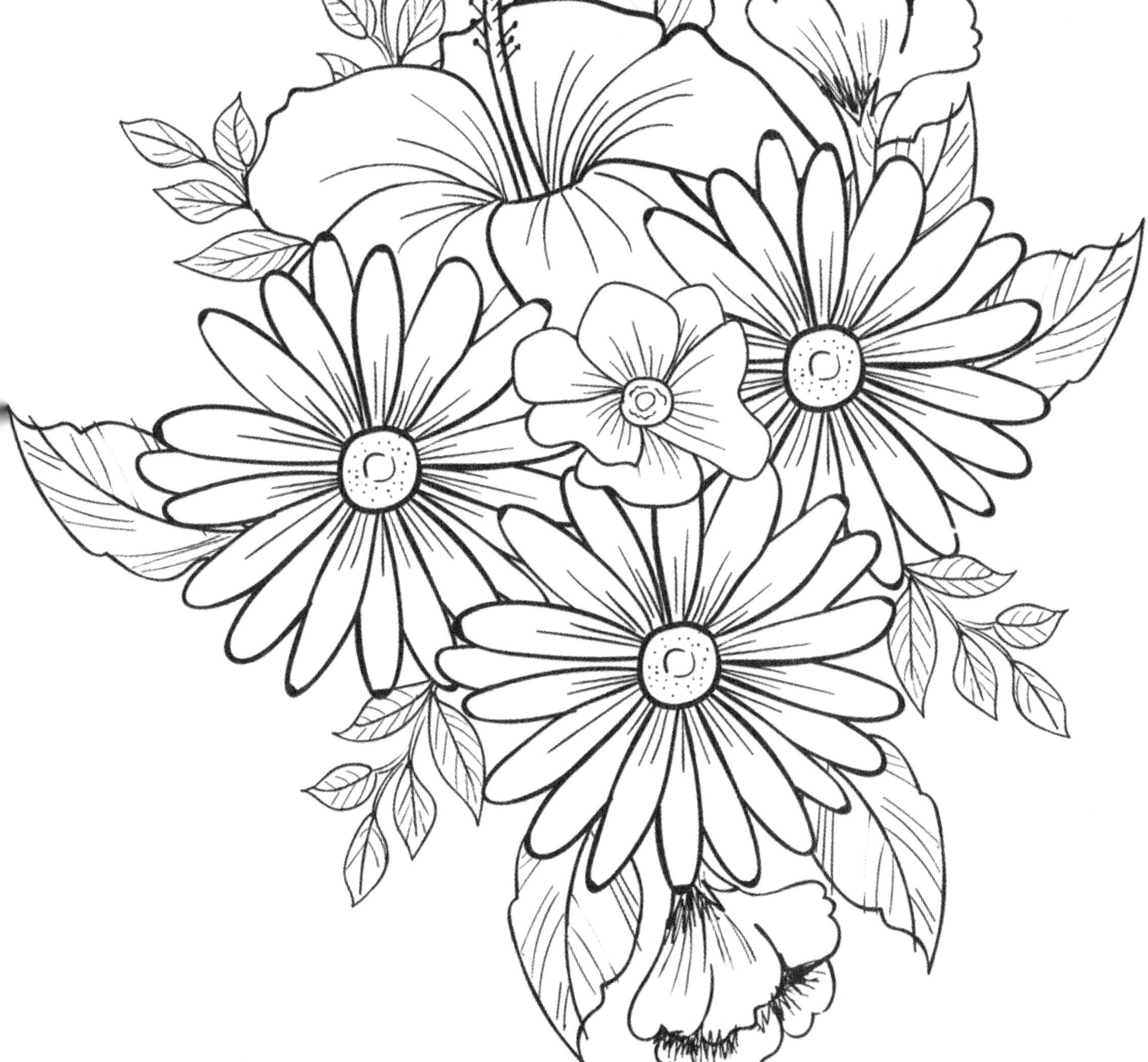

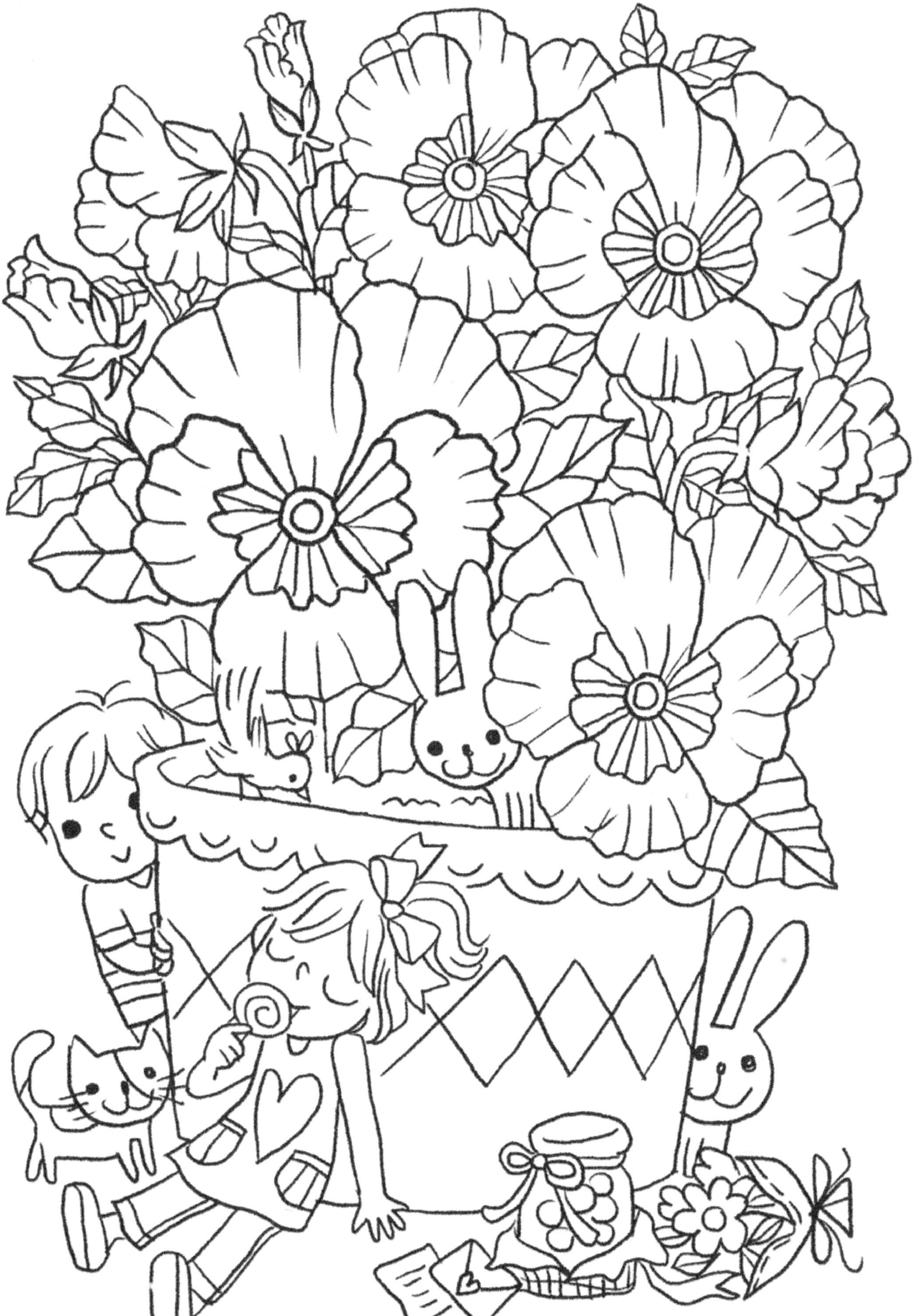

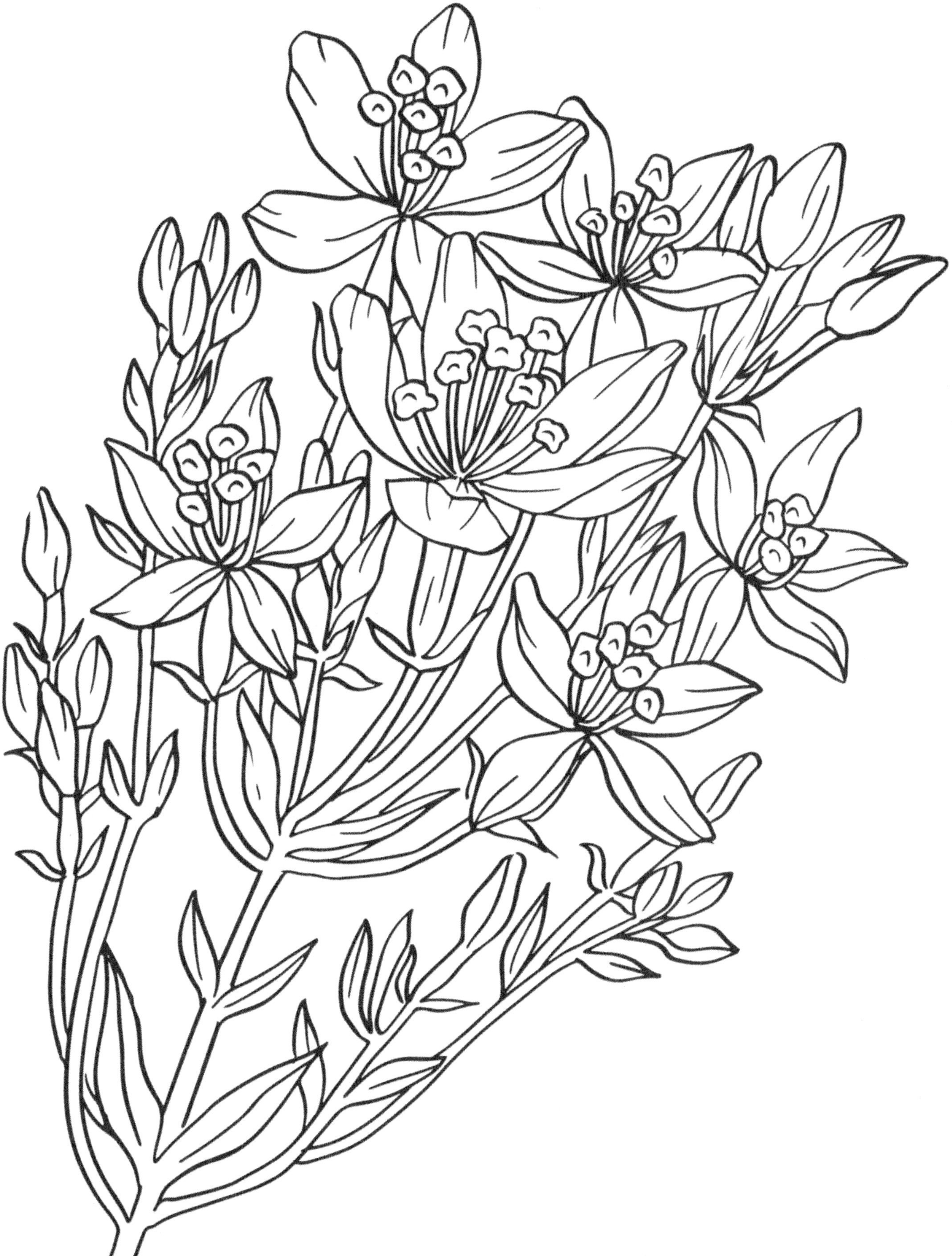

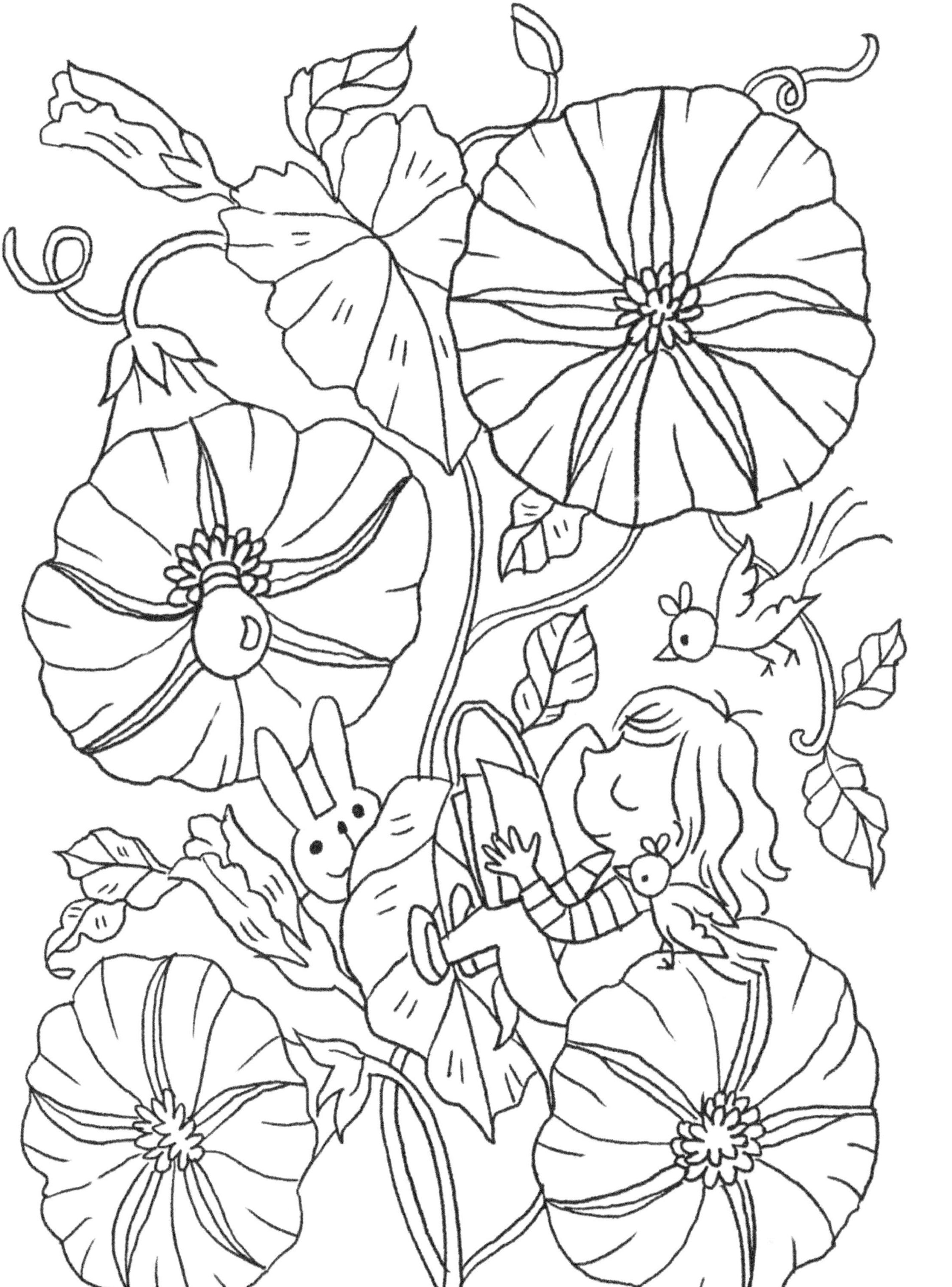

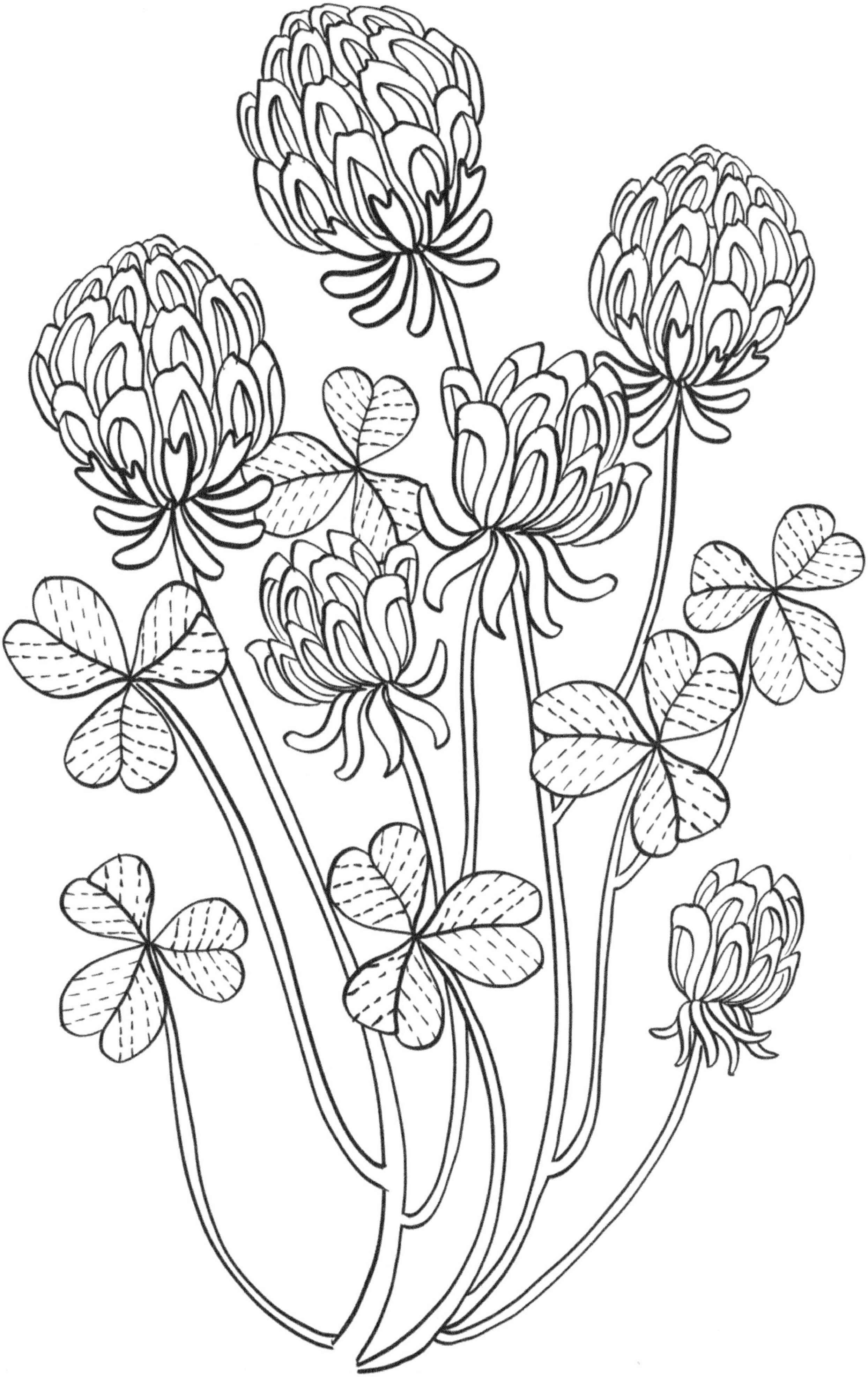

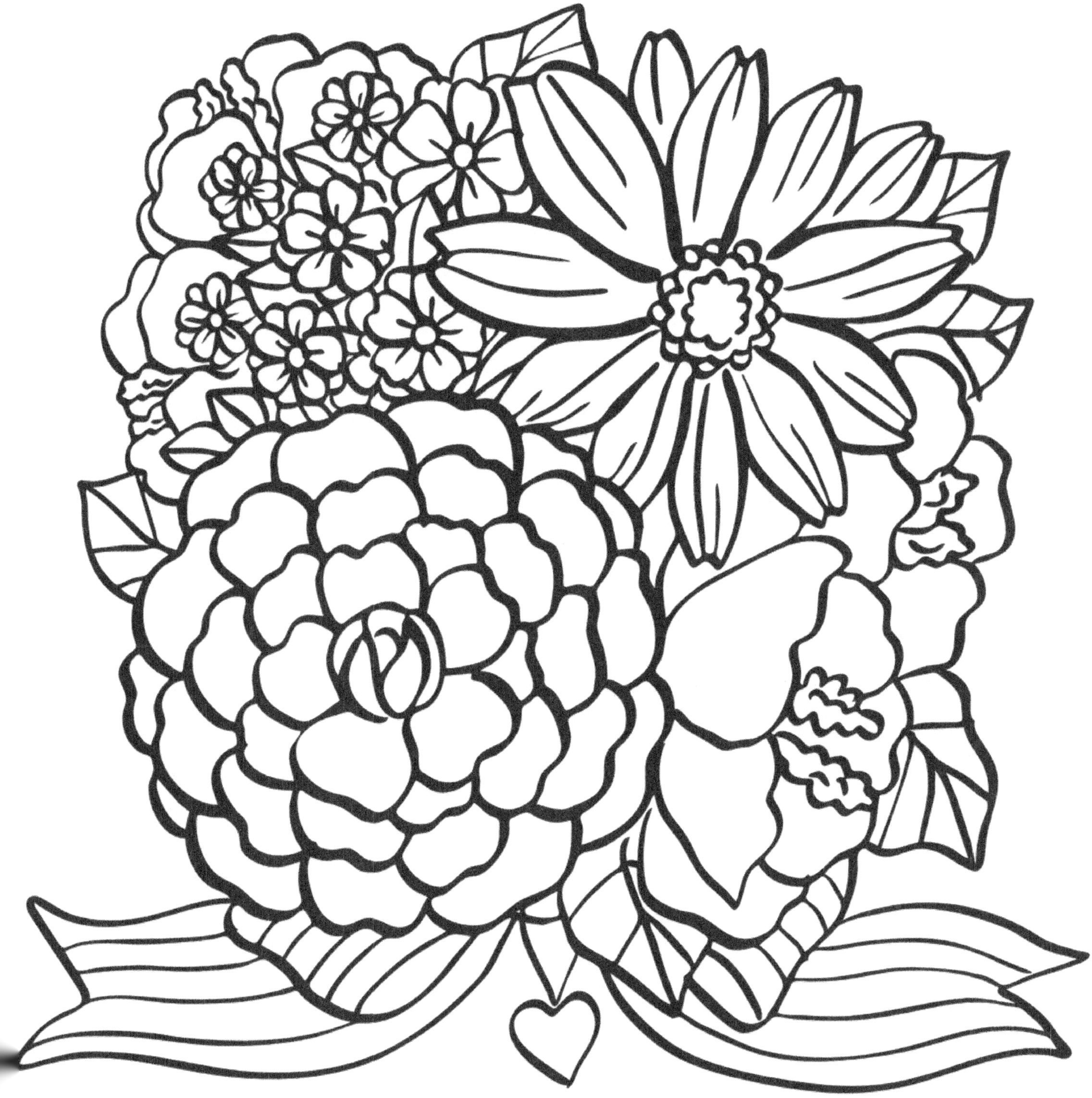

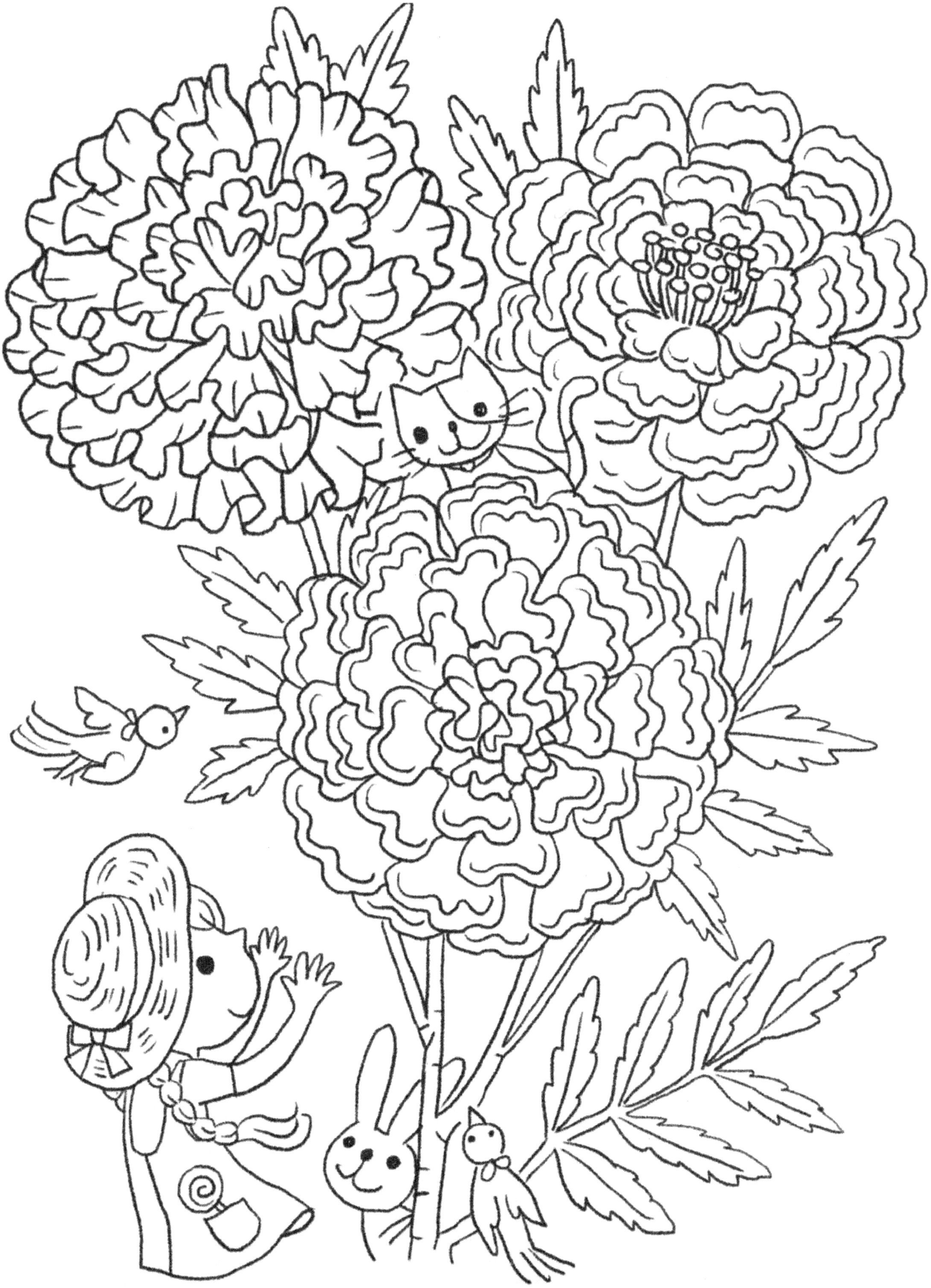

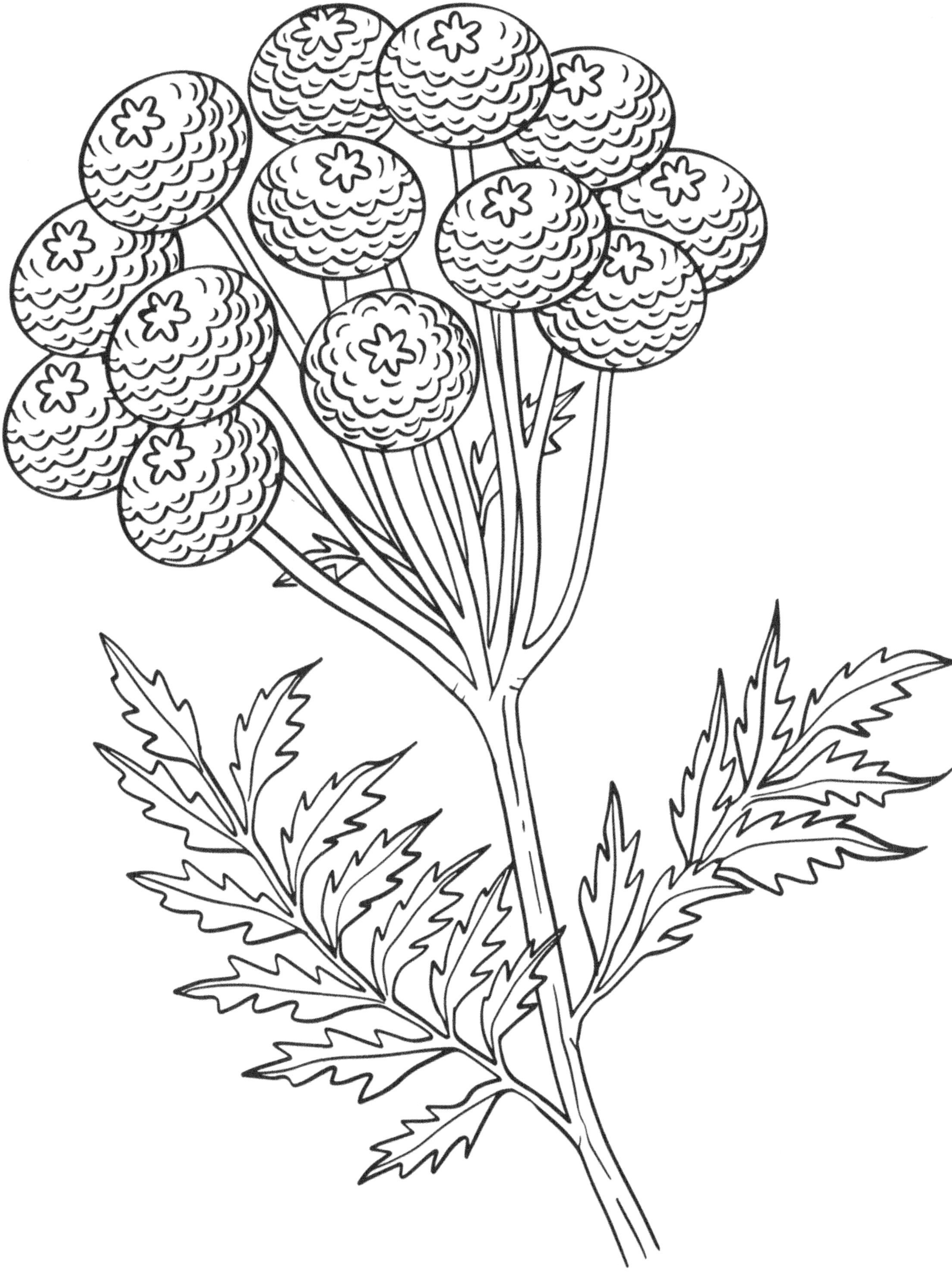

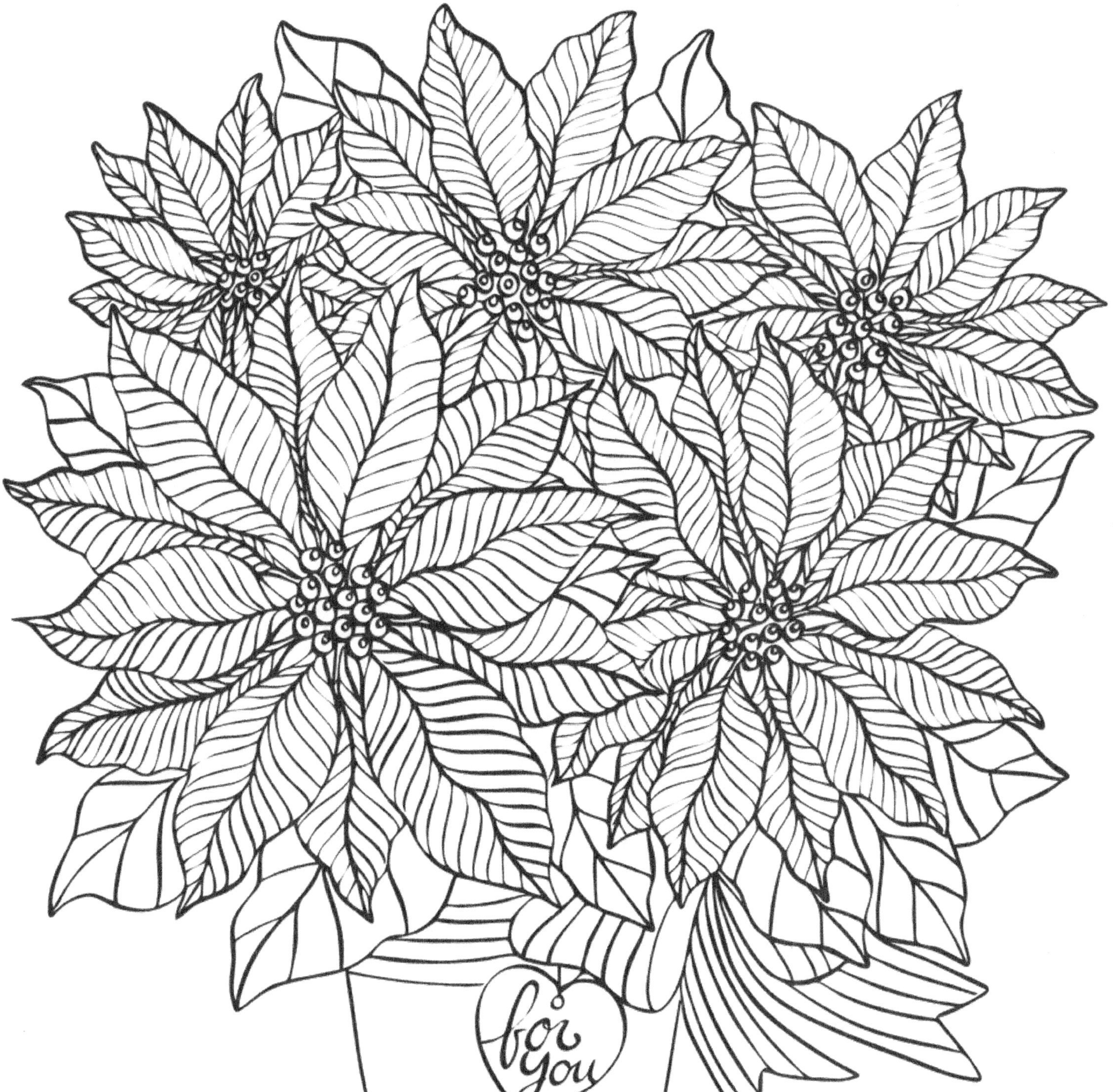
for you

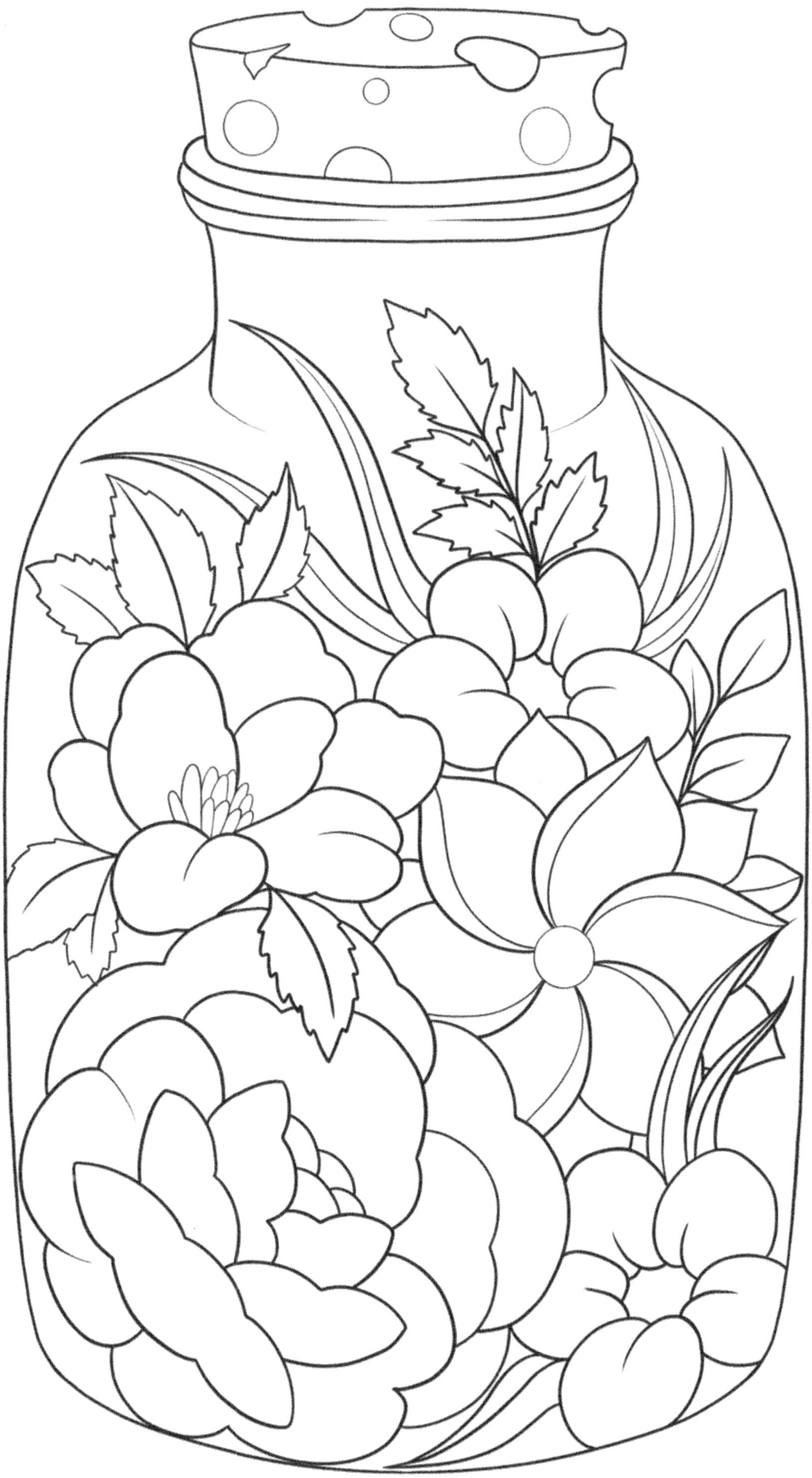

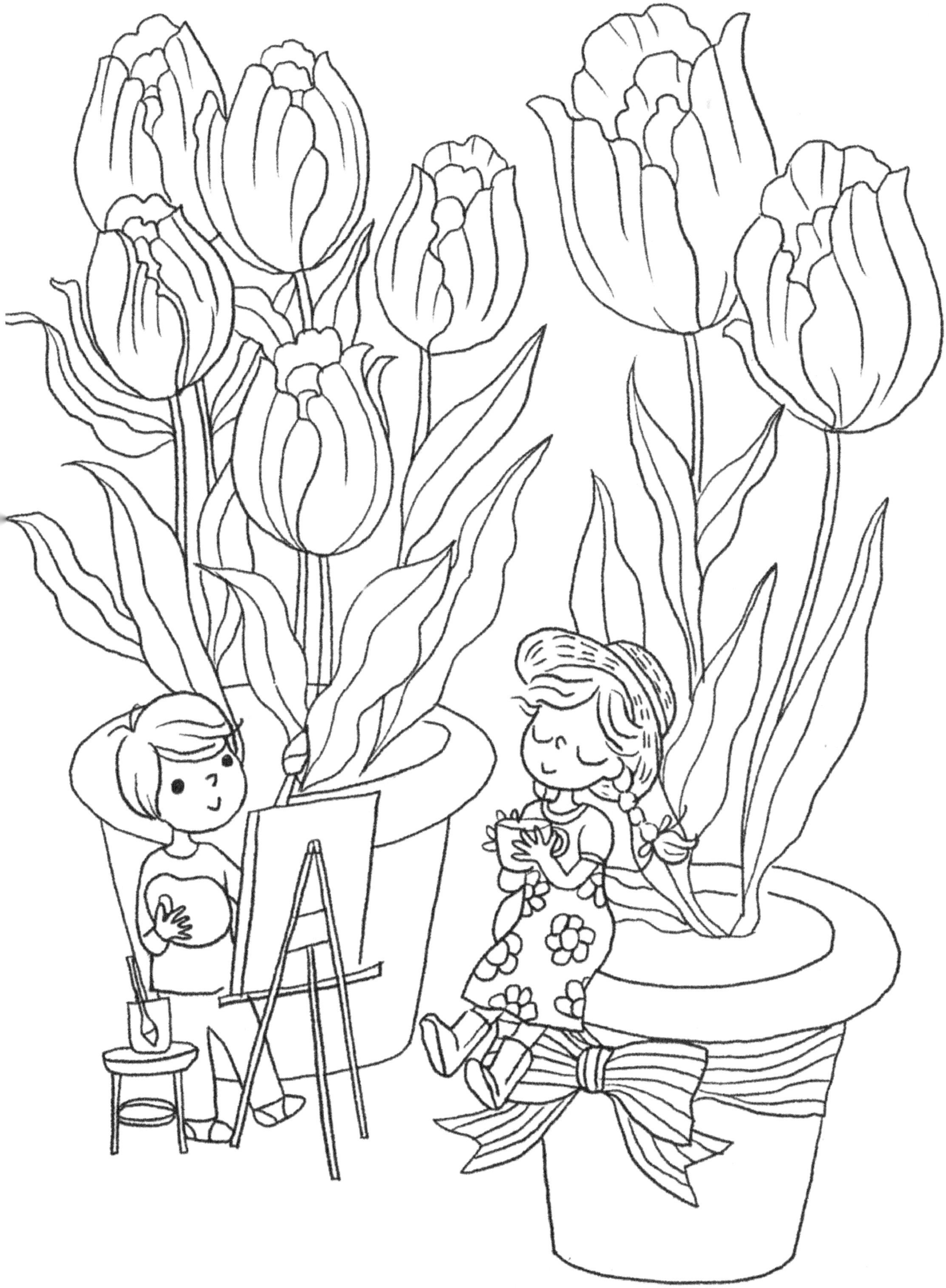

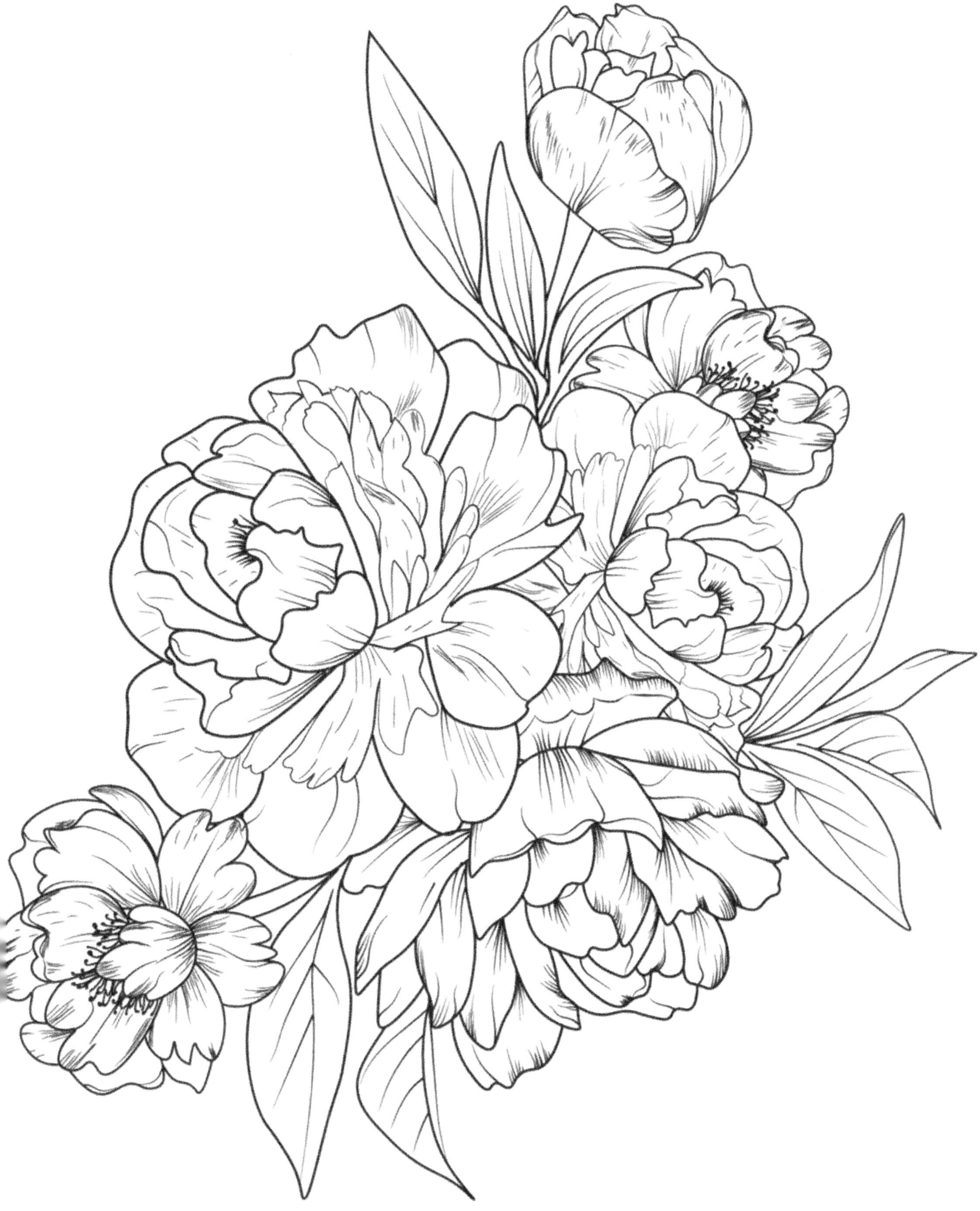

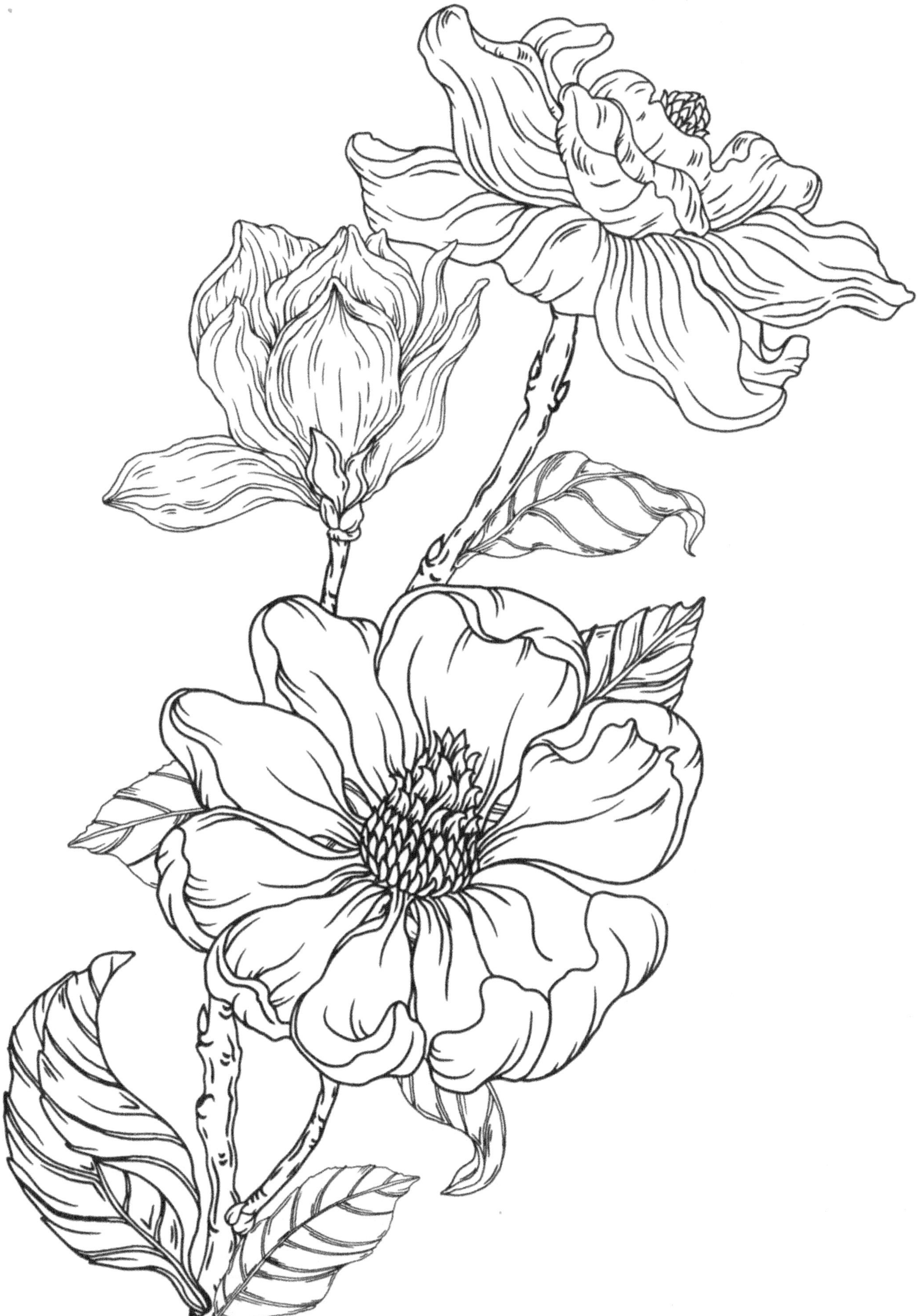

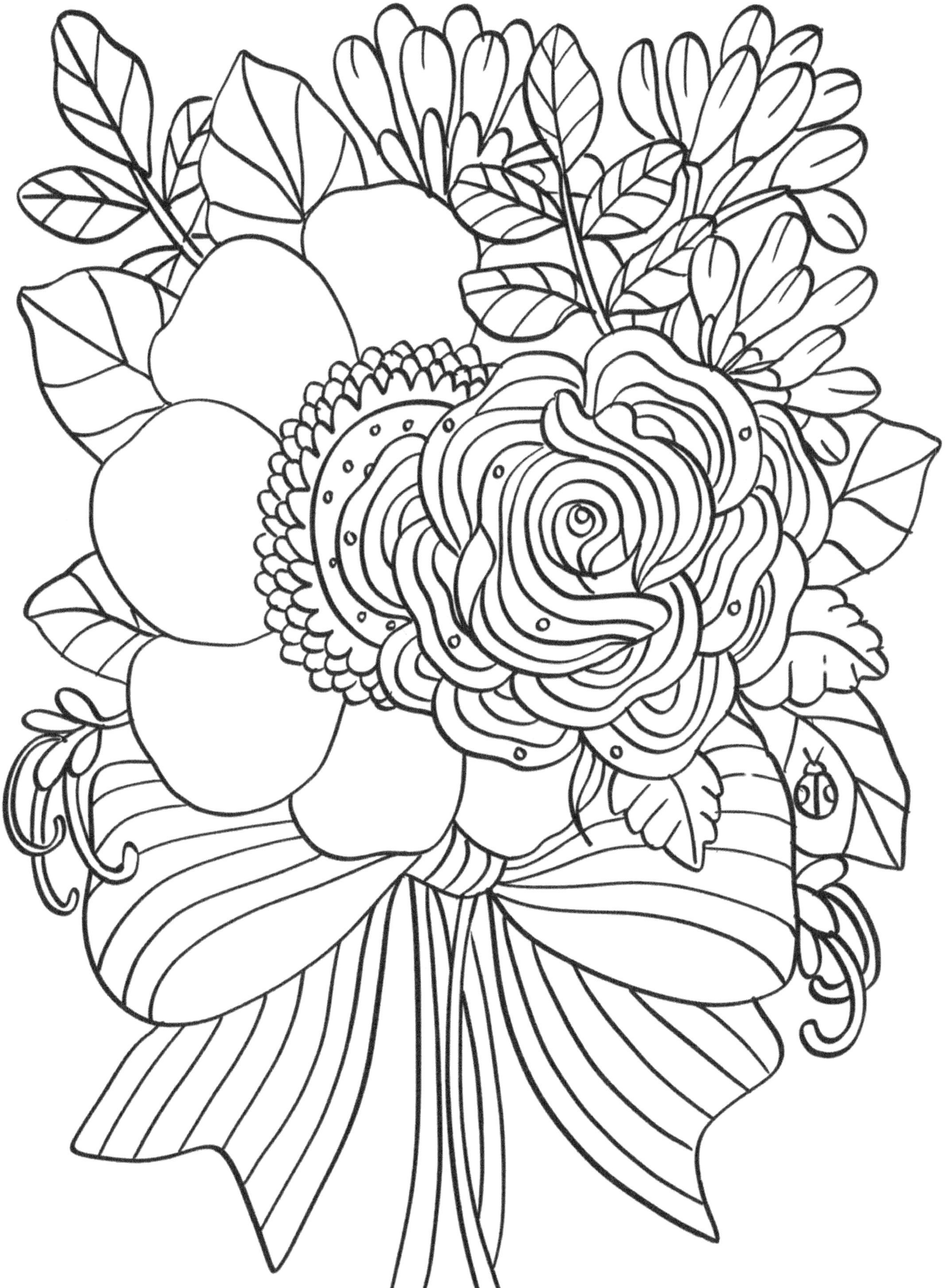

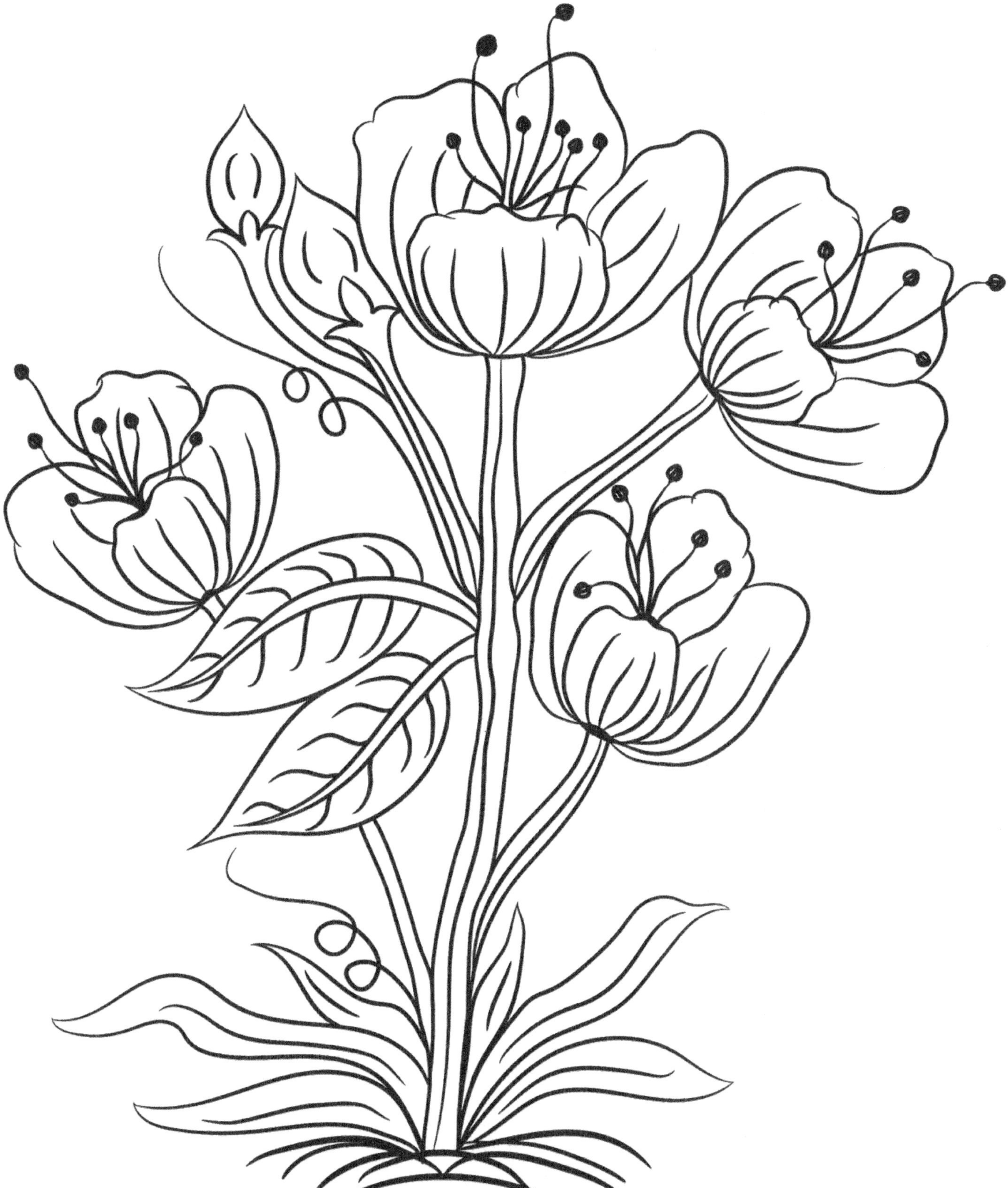

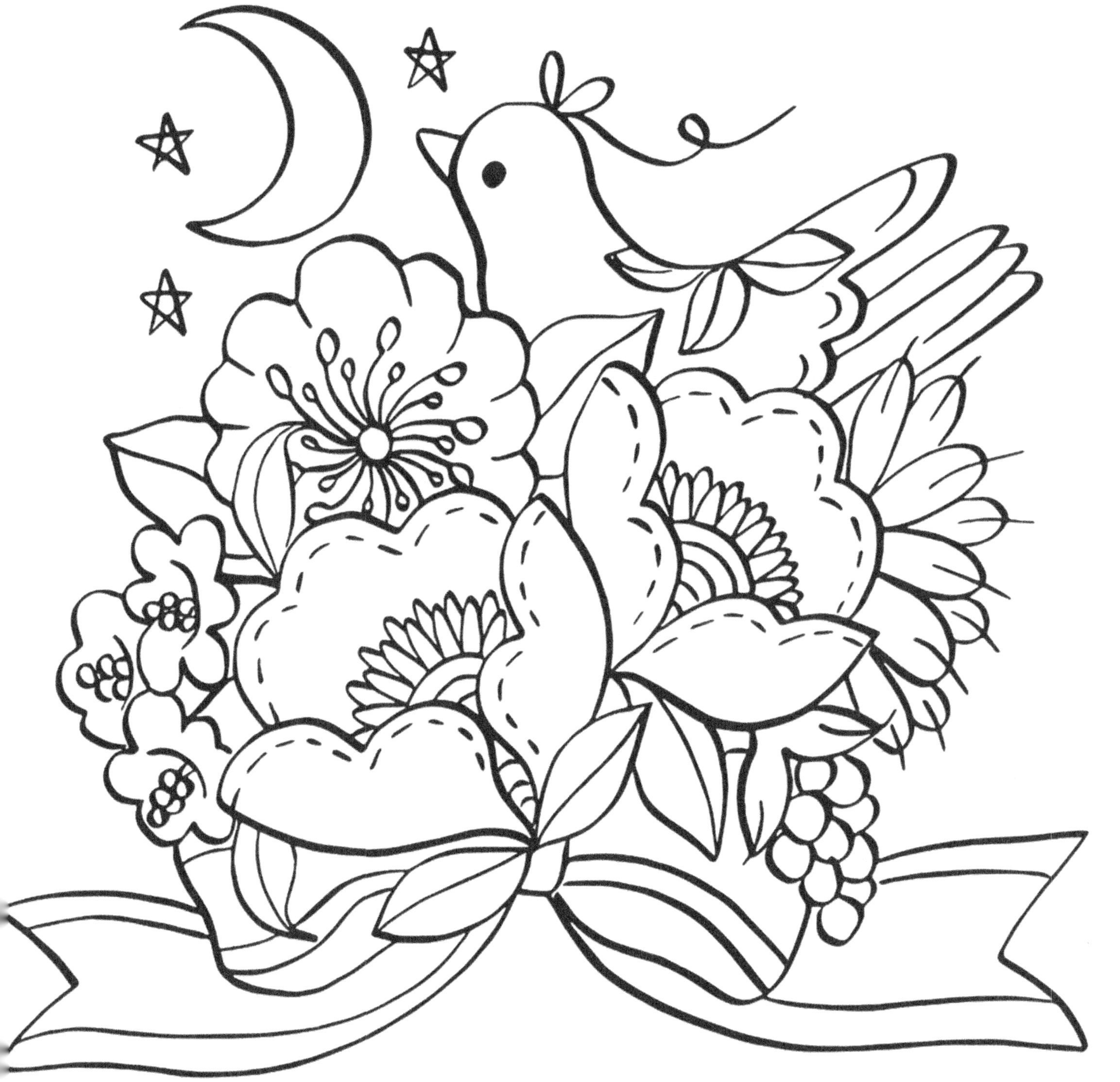

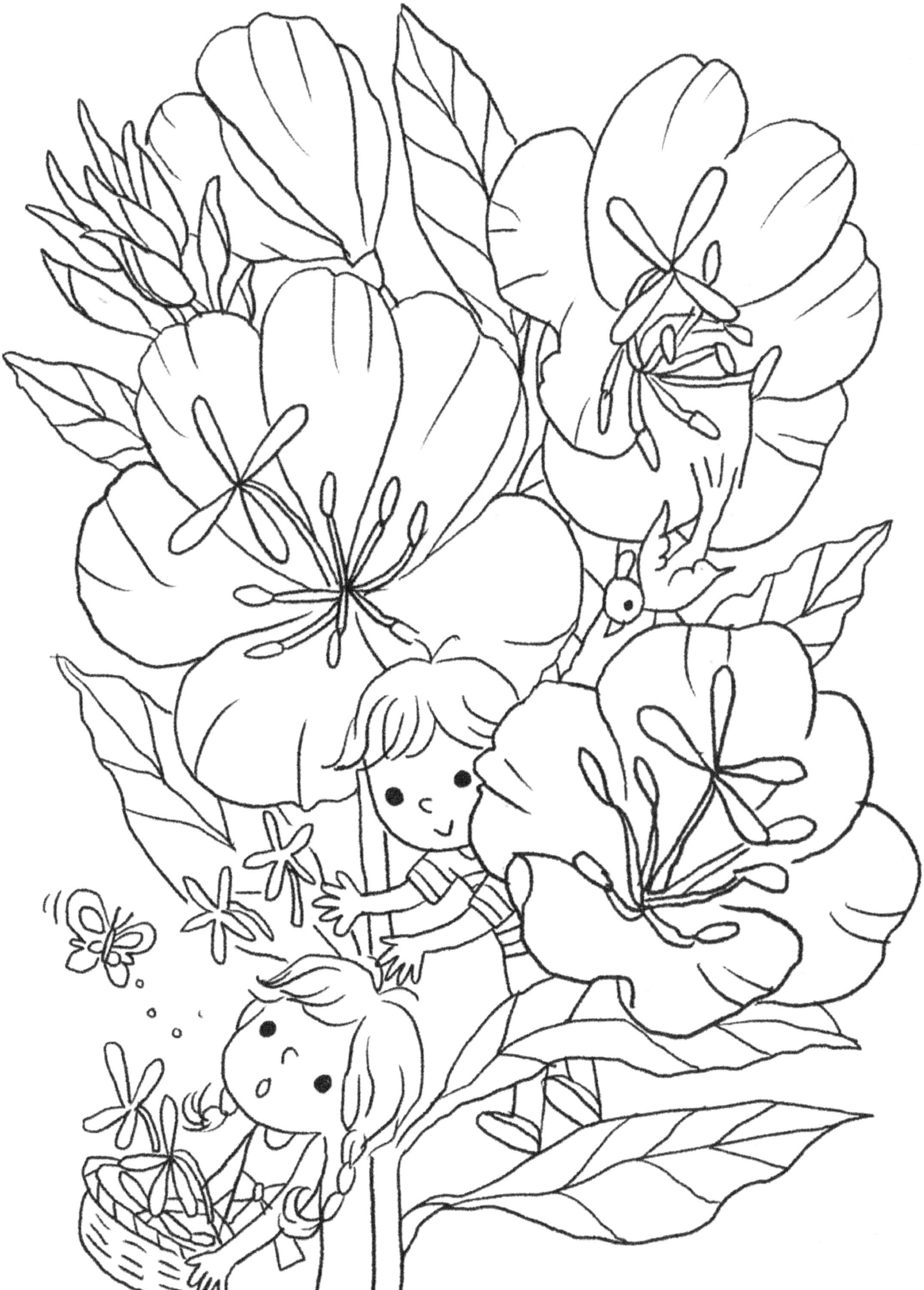

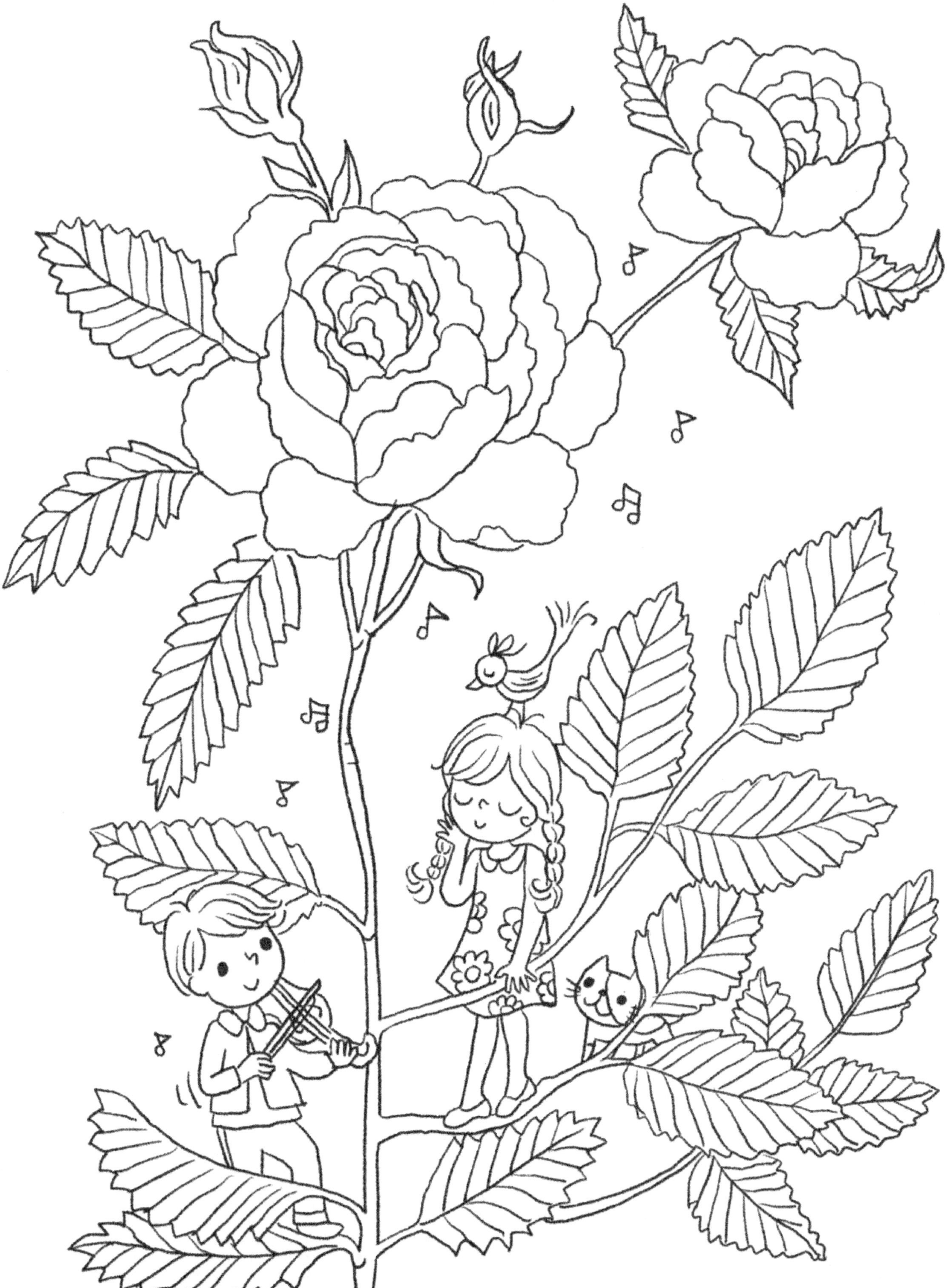

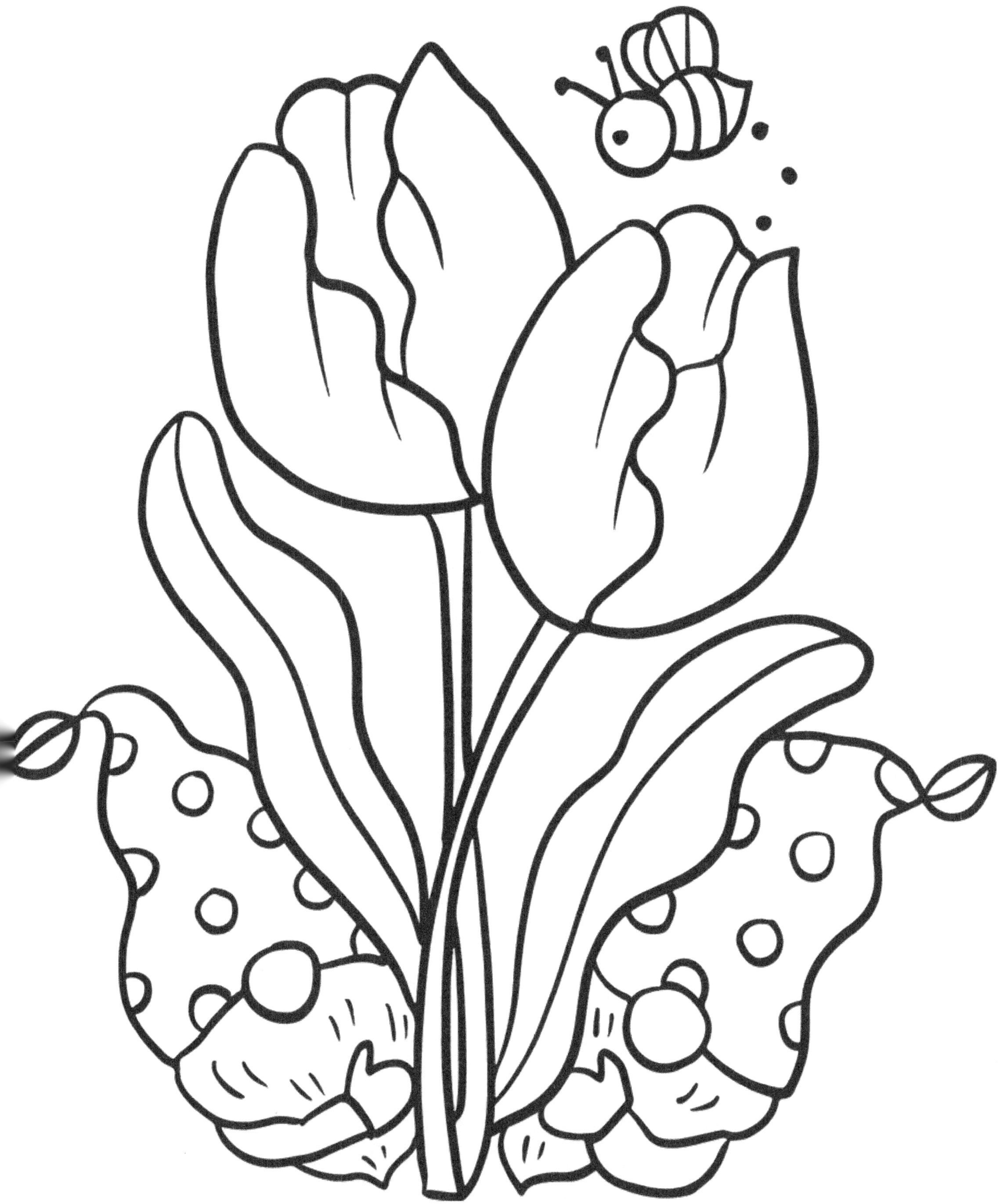

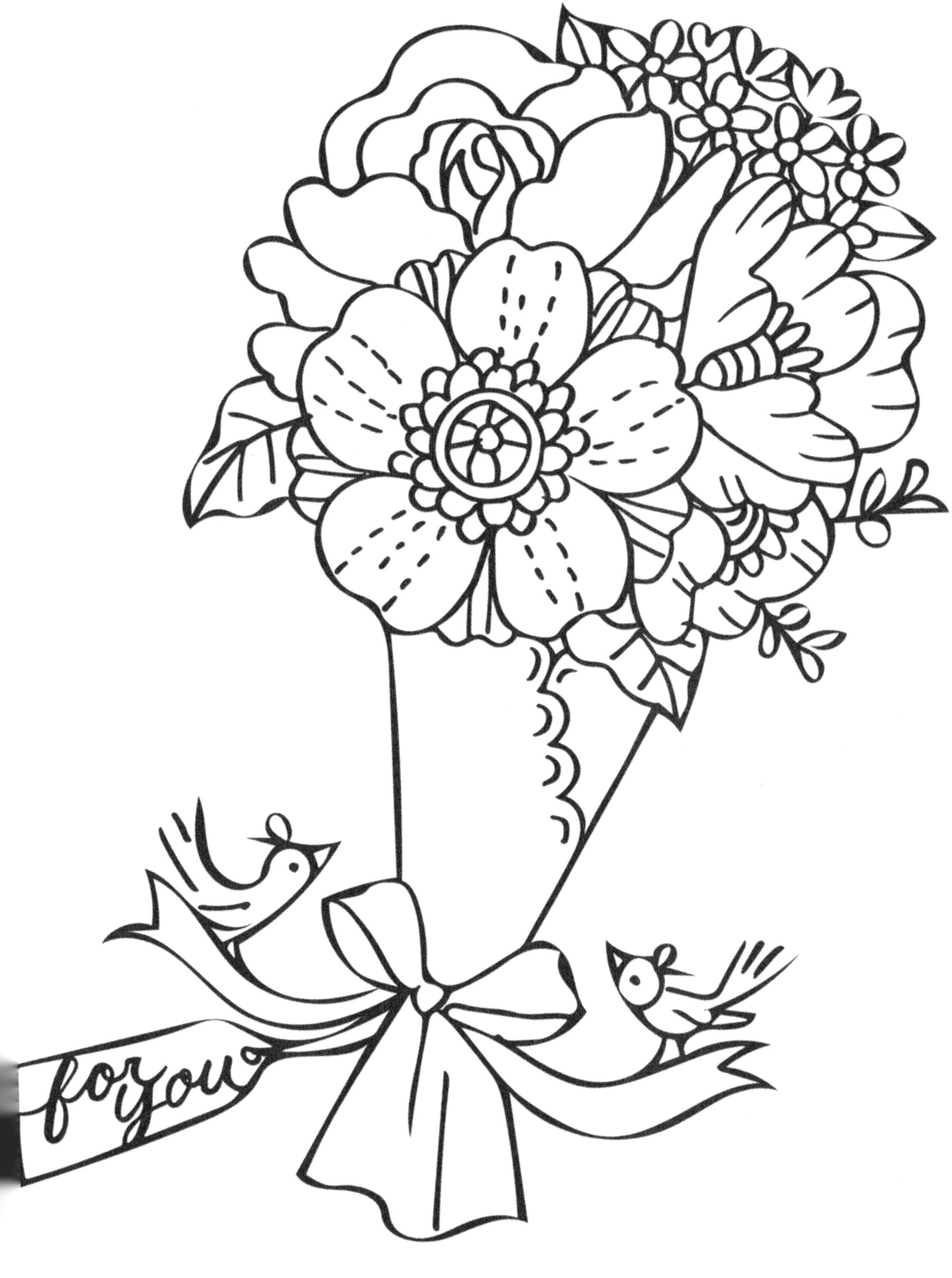
for you

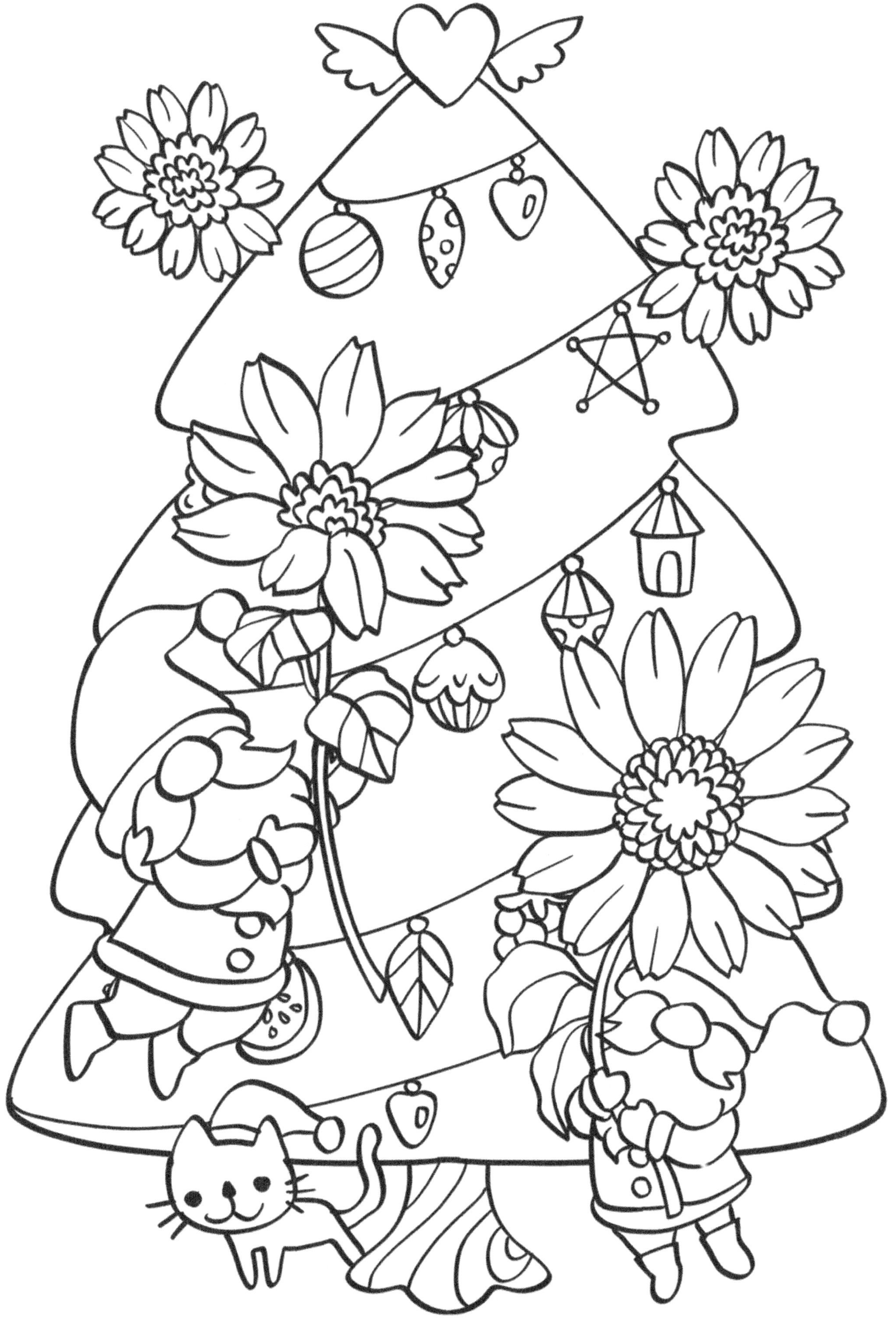

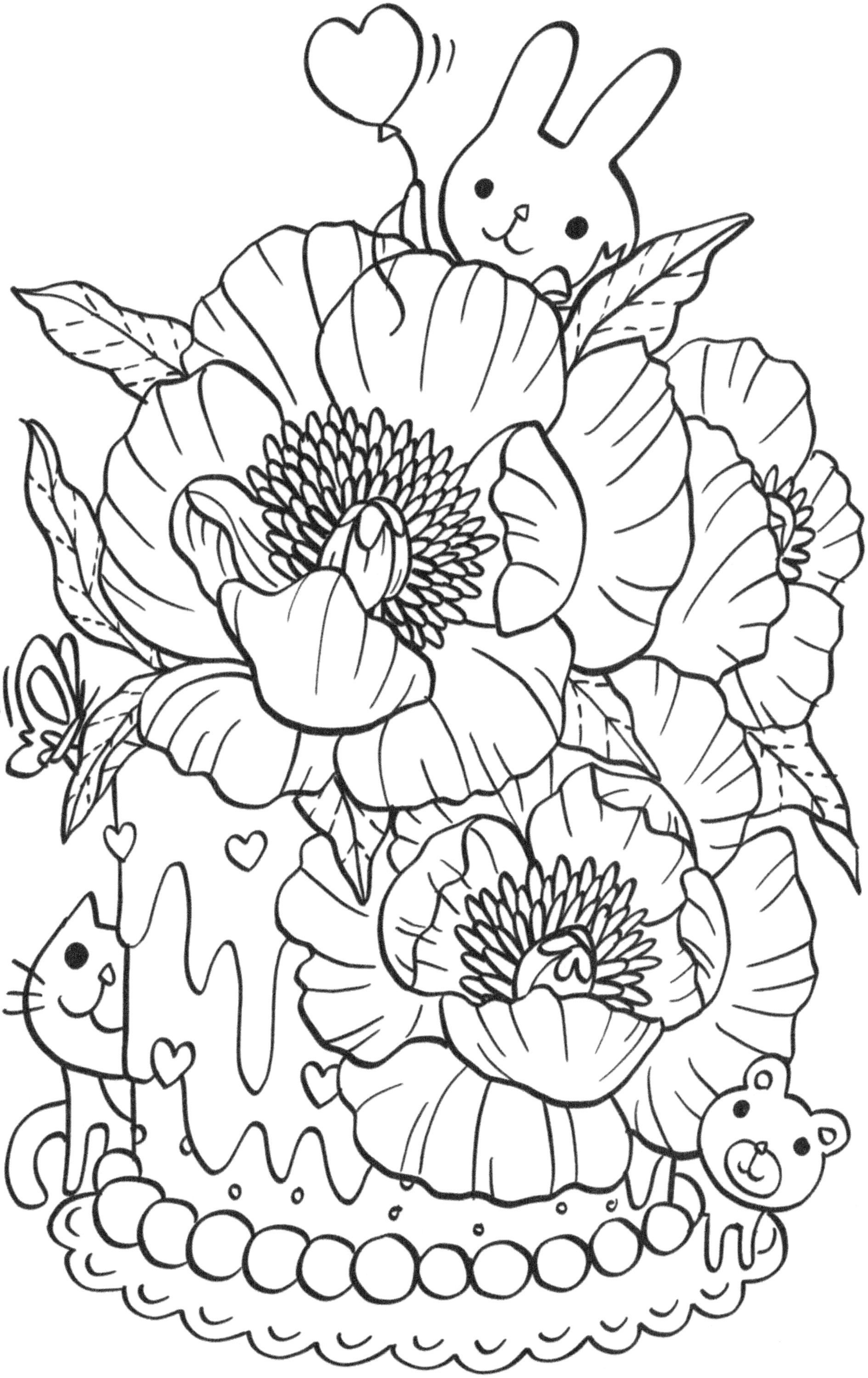

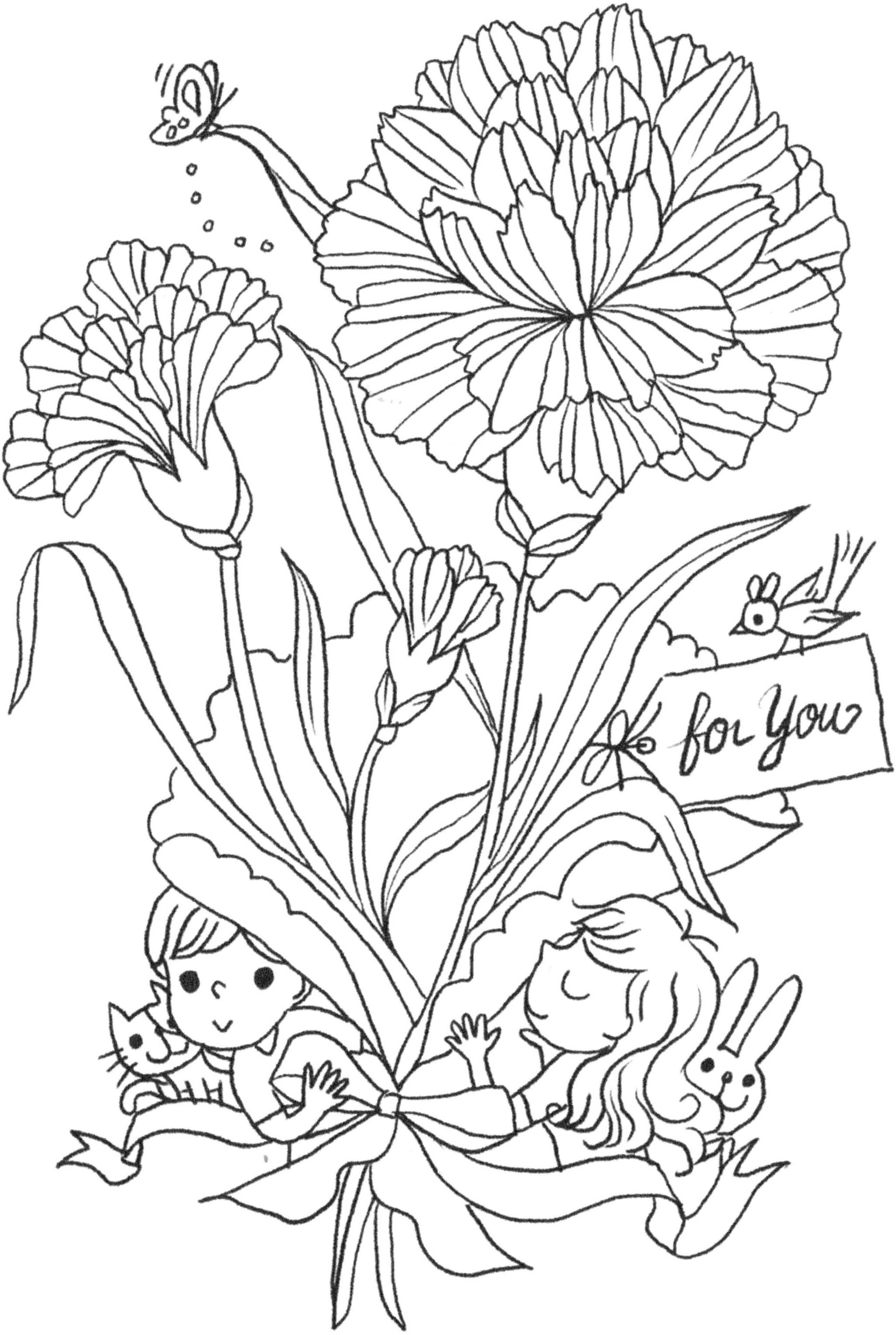
for you

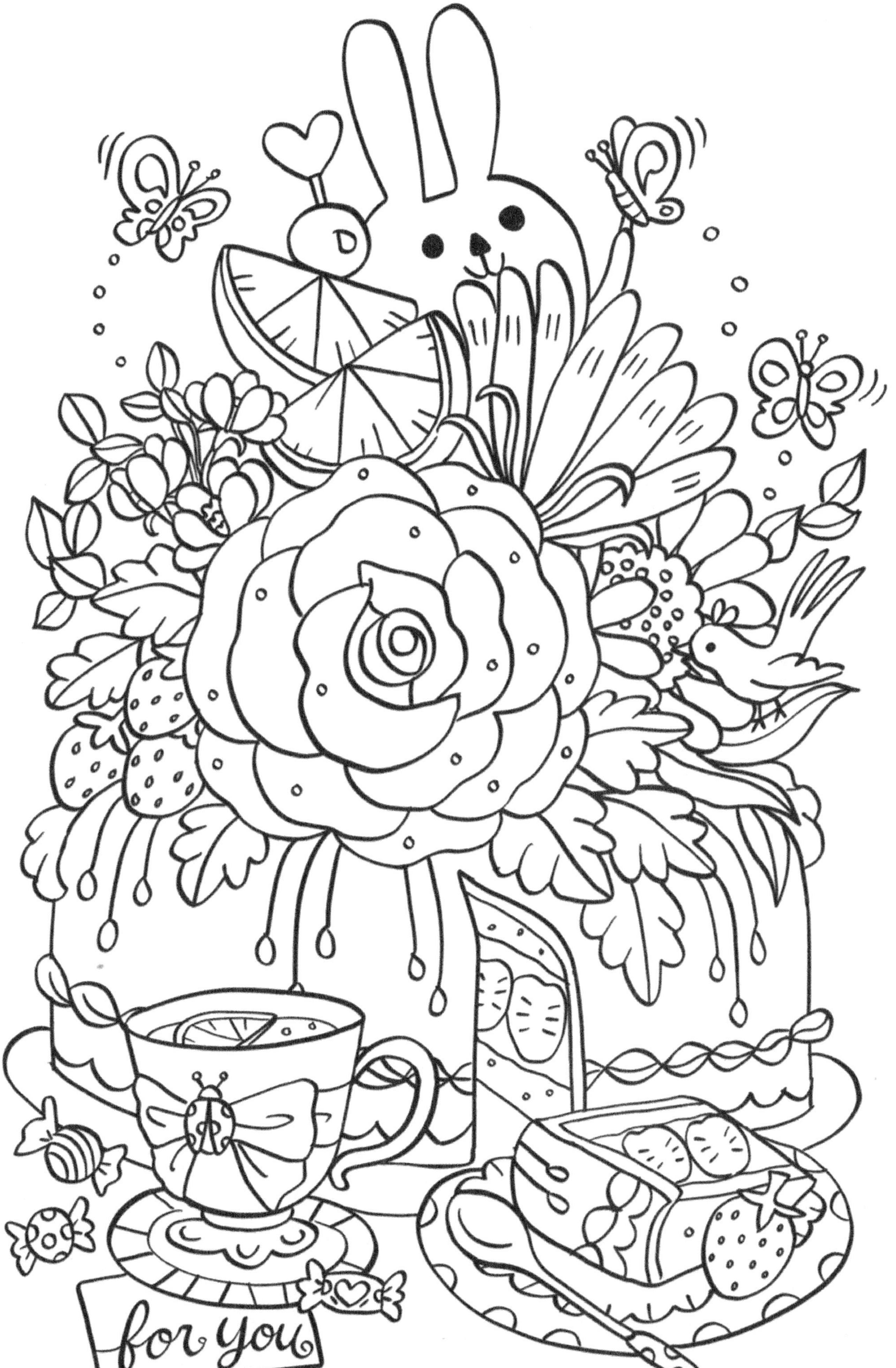
for you

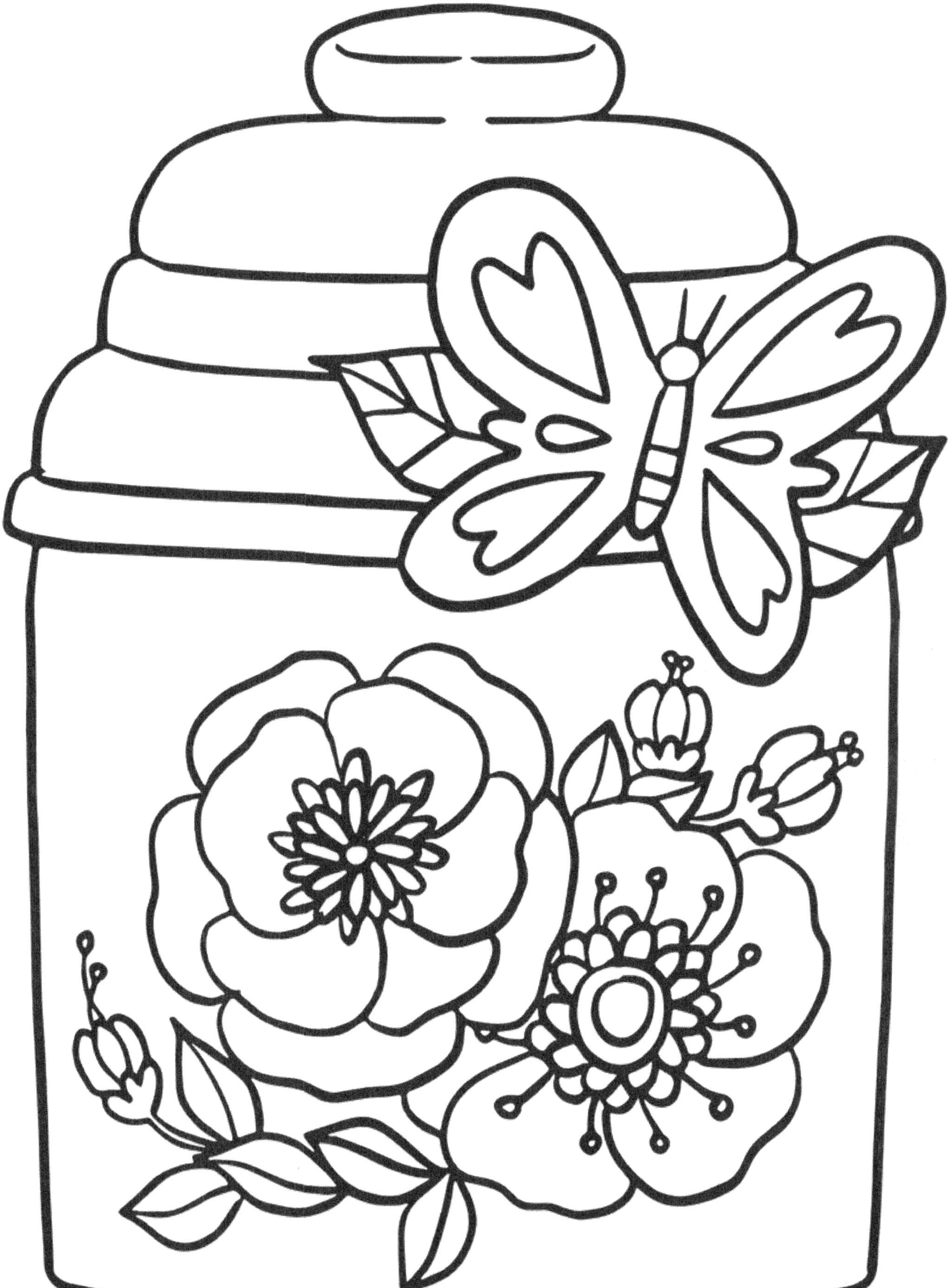

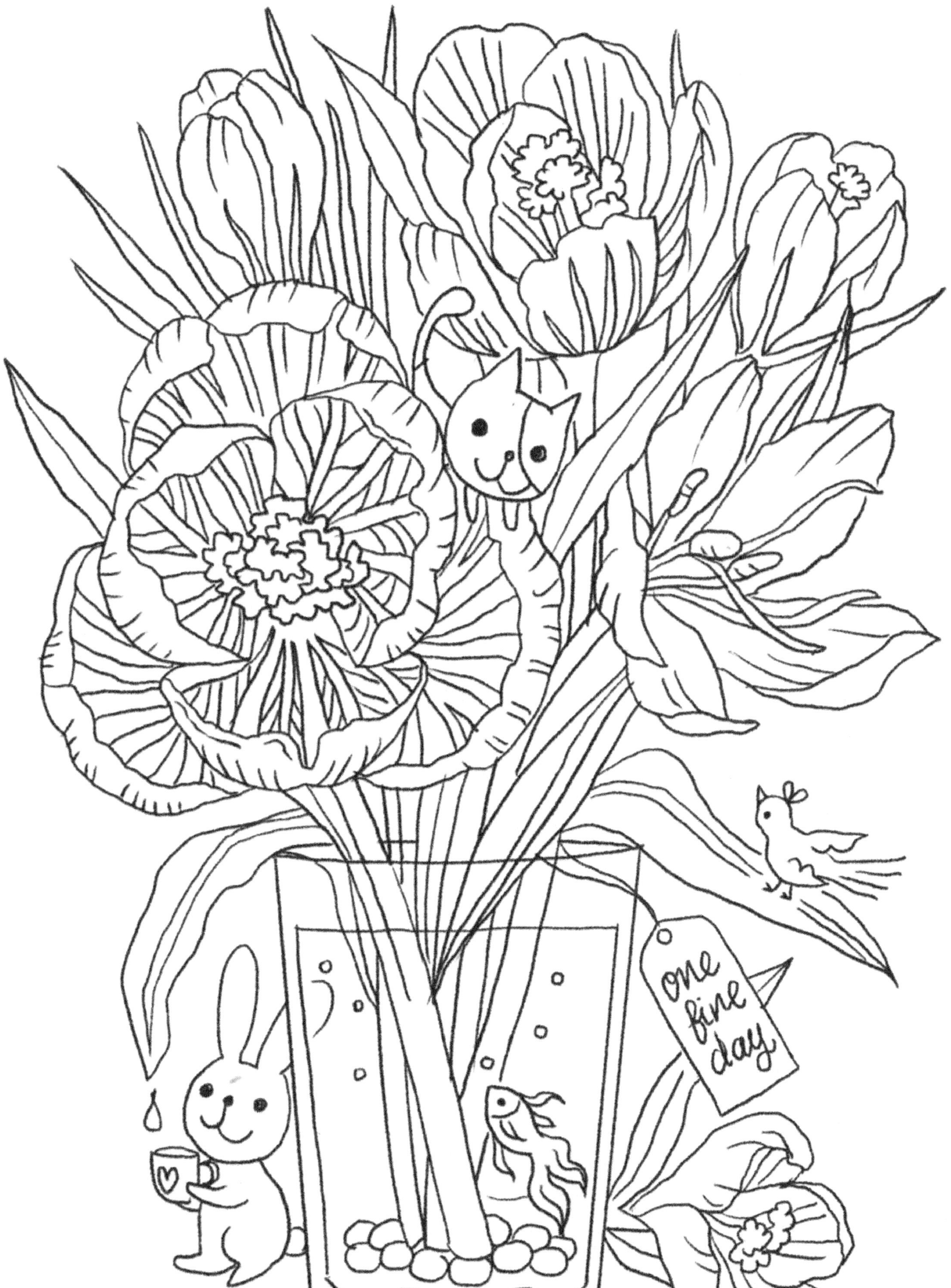
one fine day

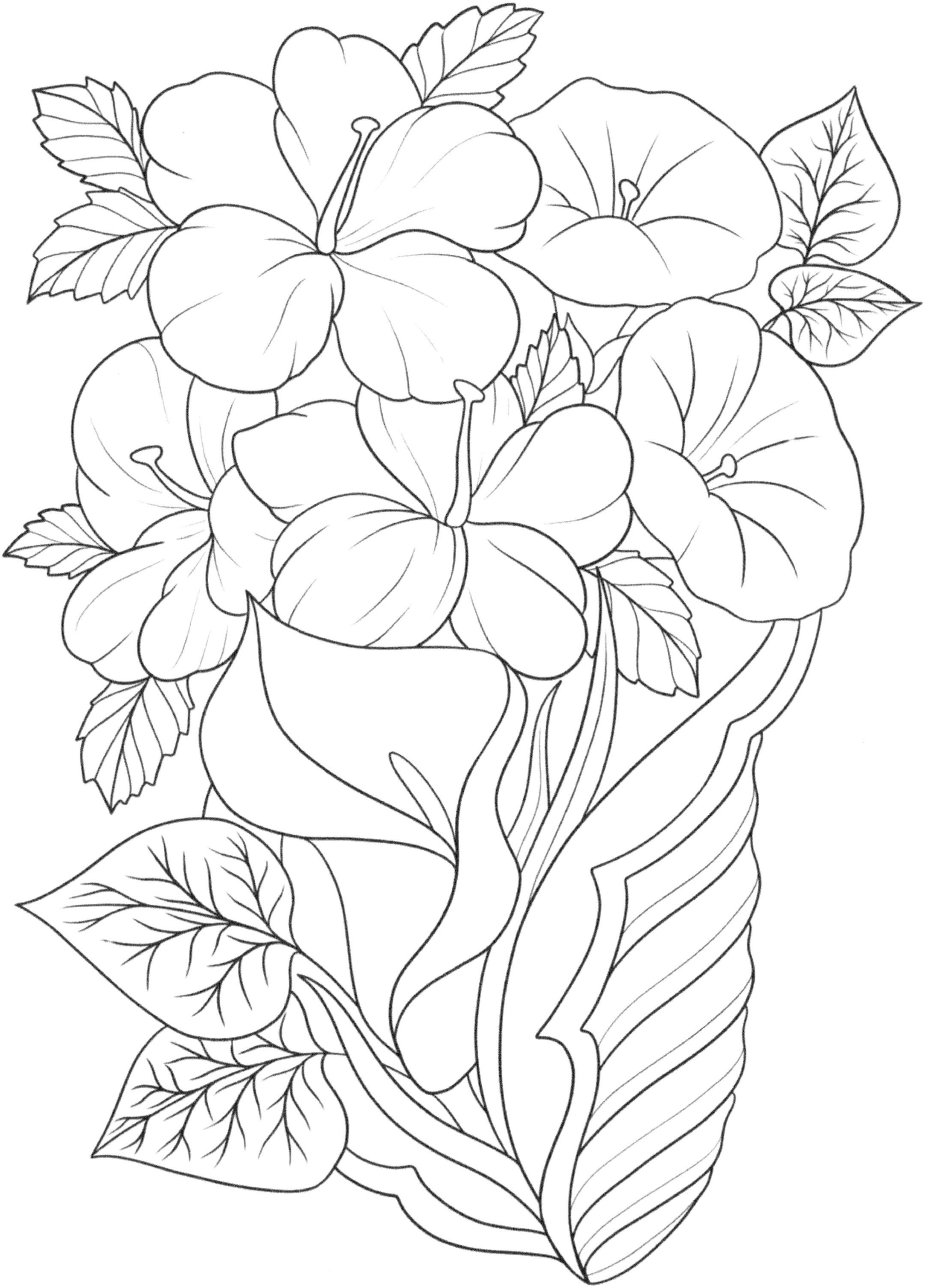

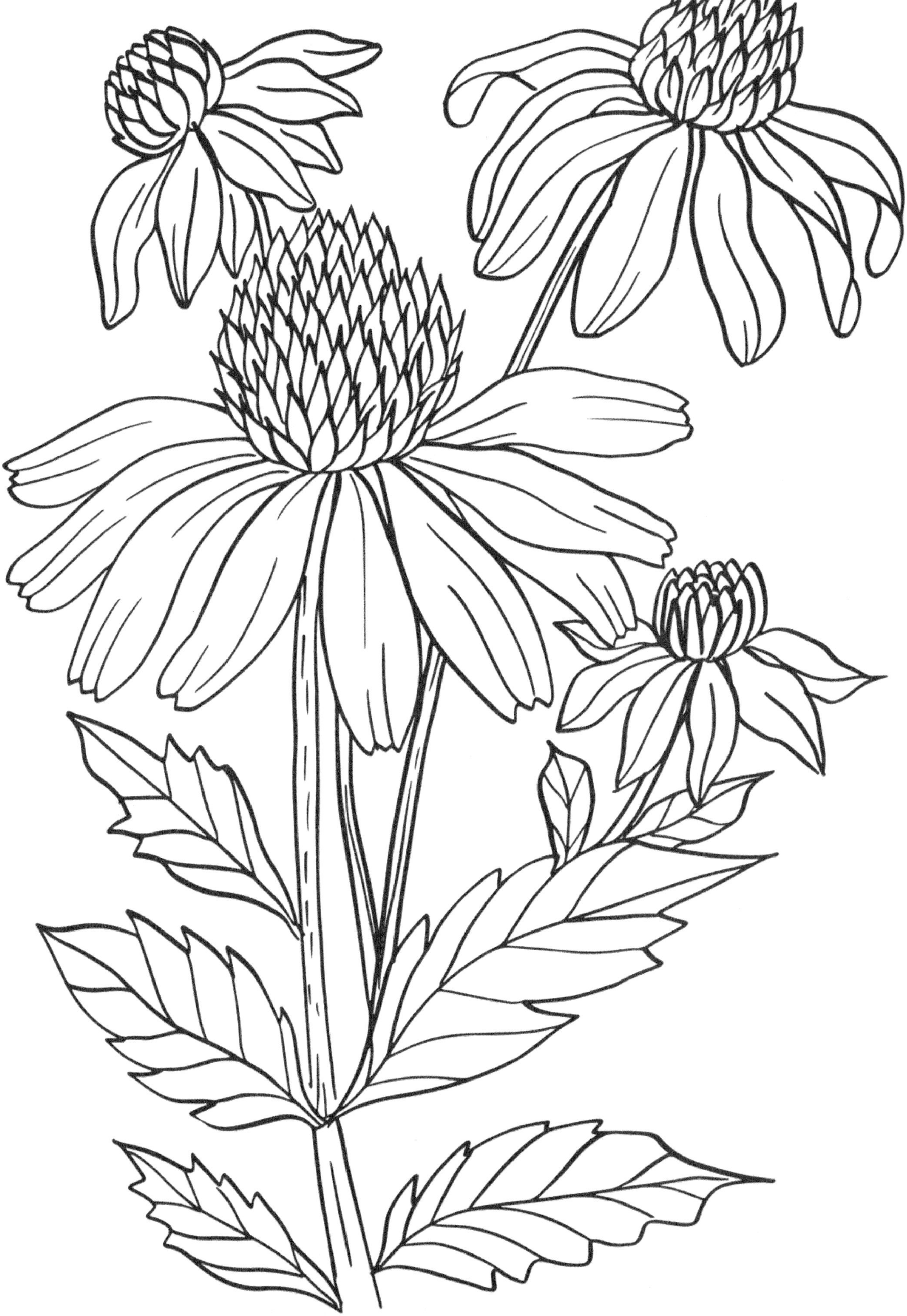

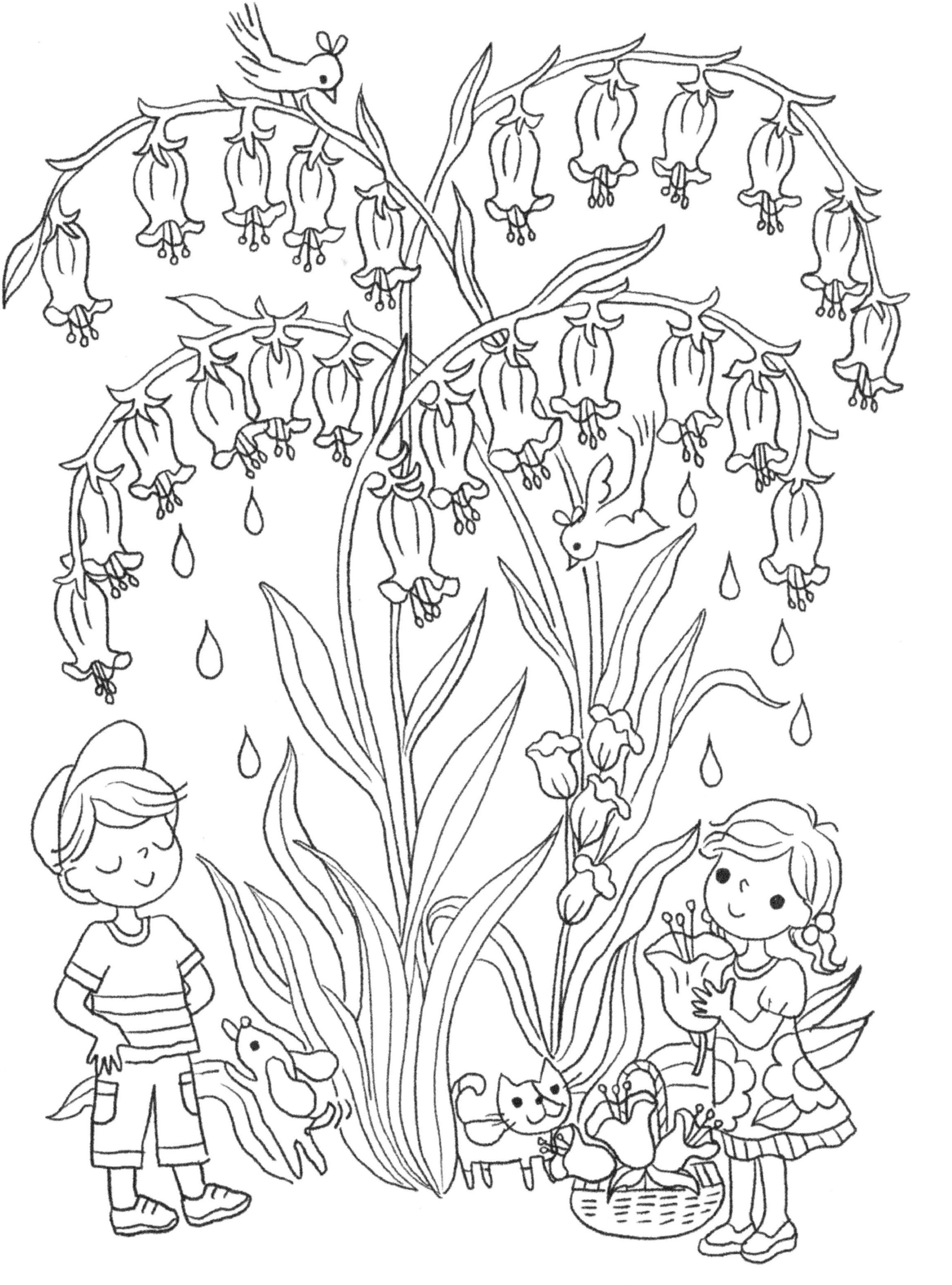

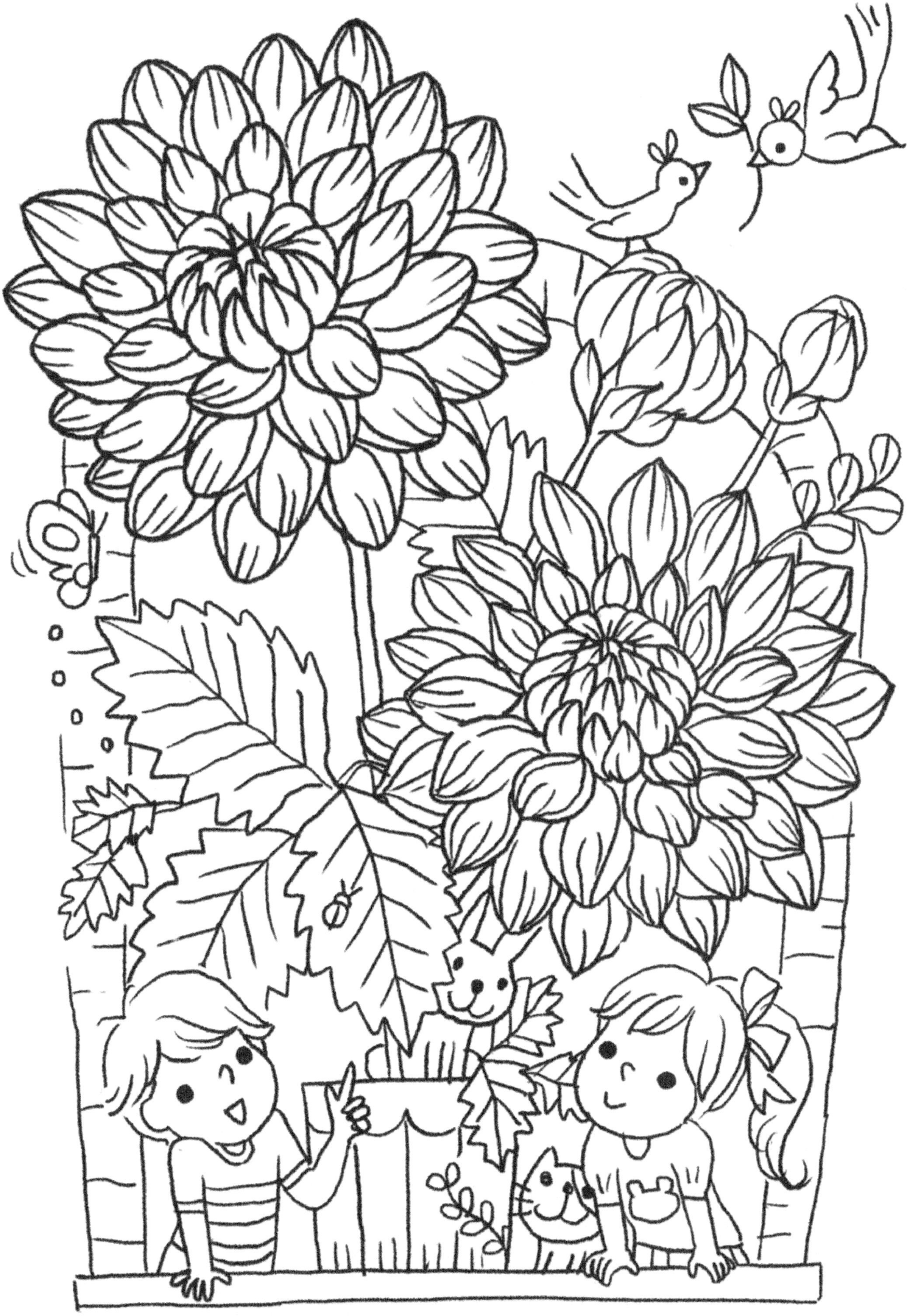

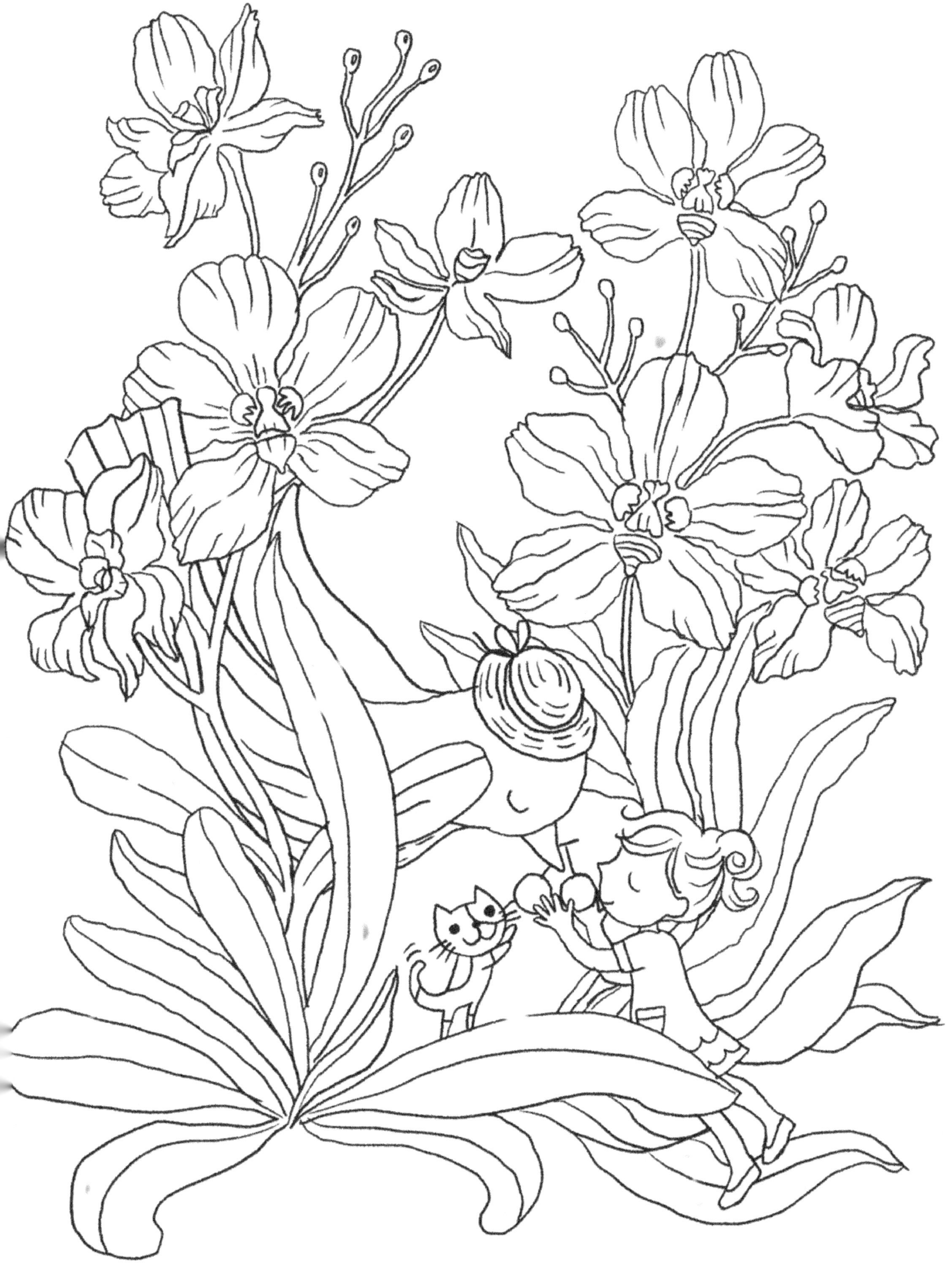

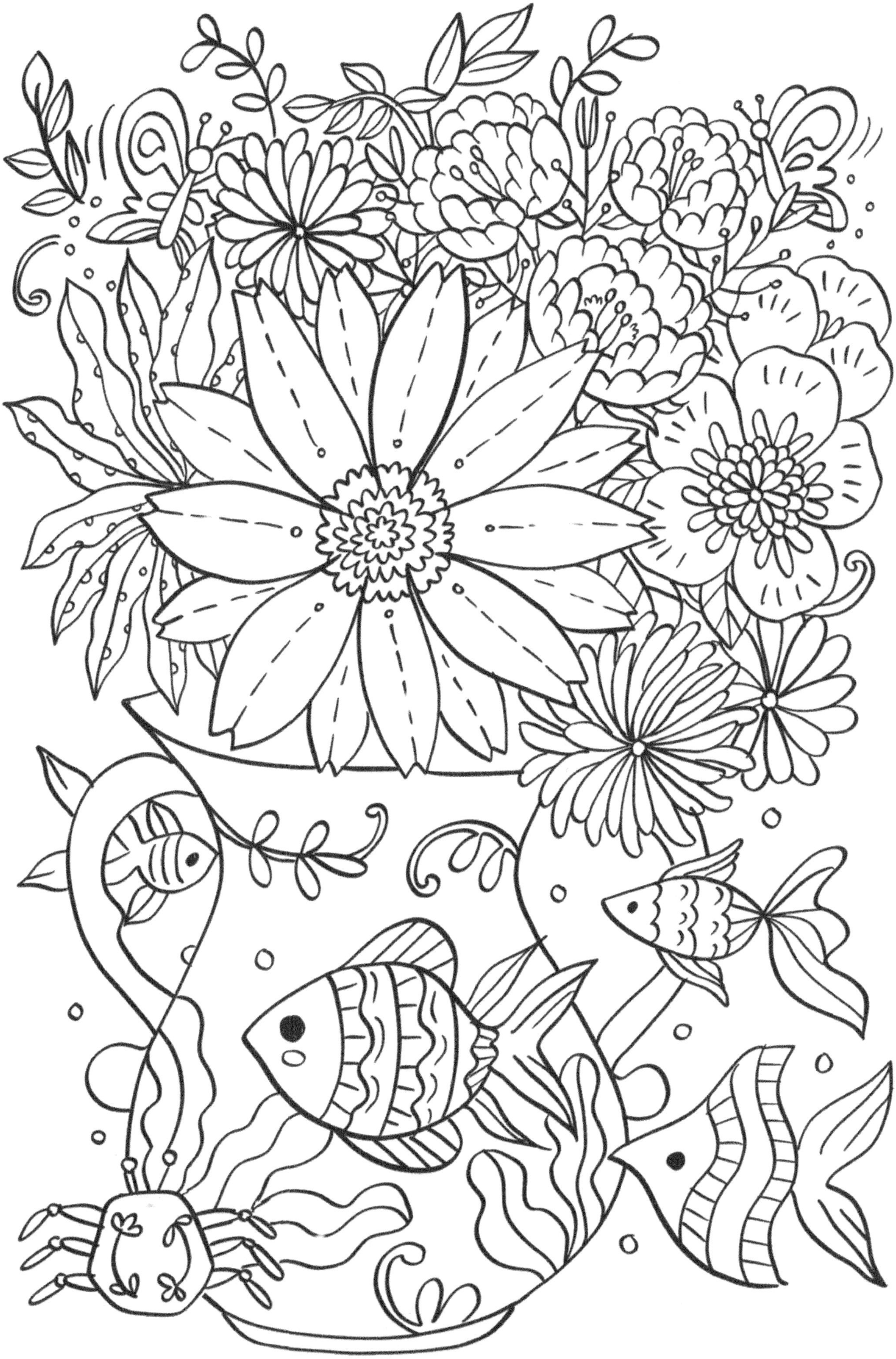

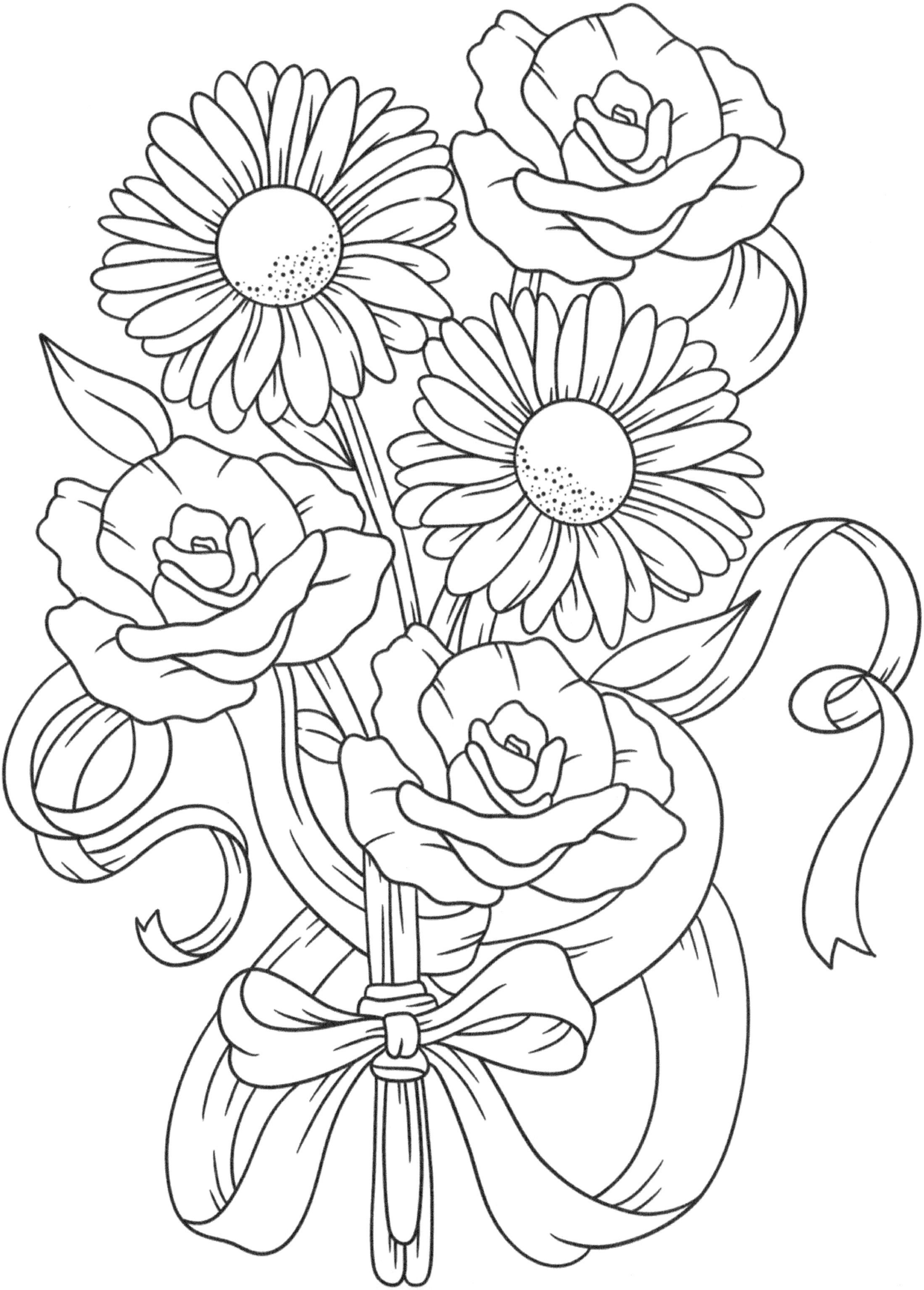

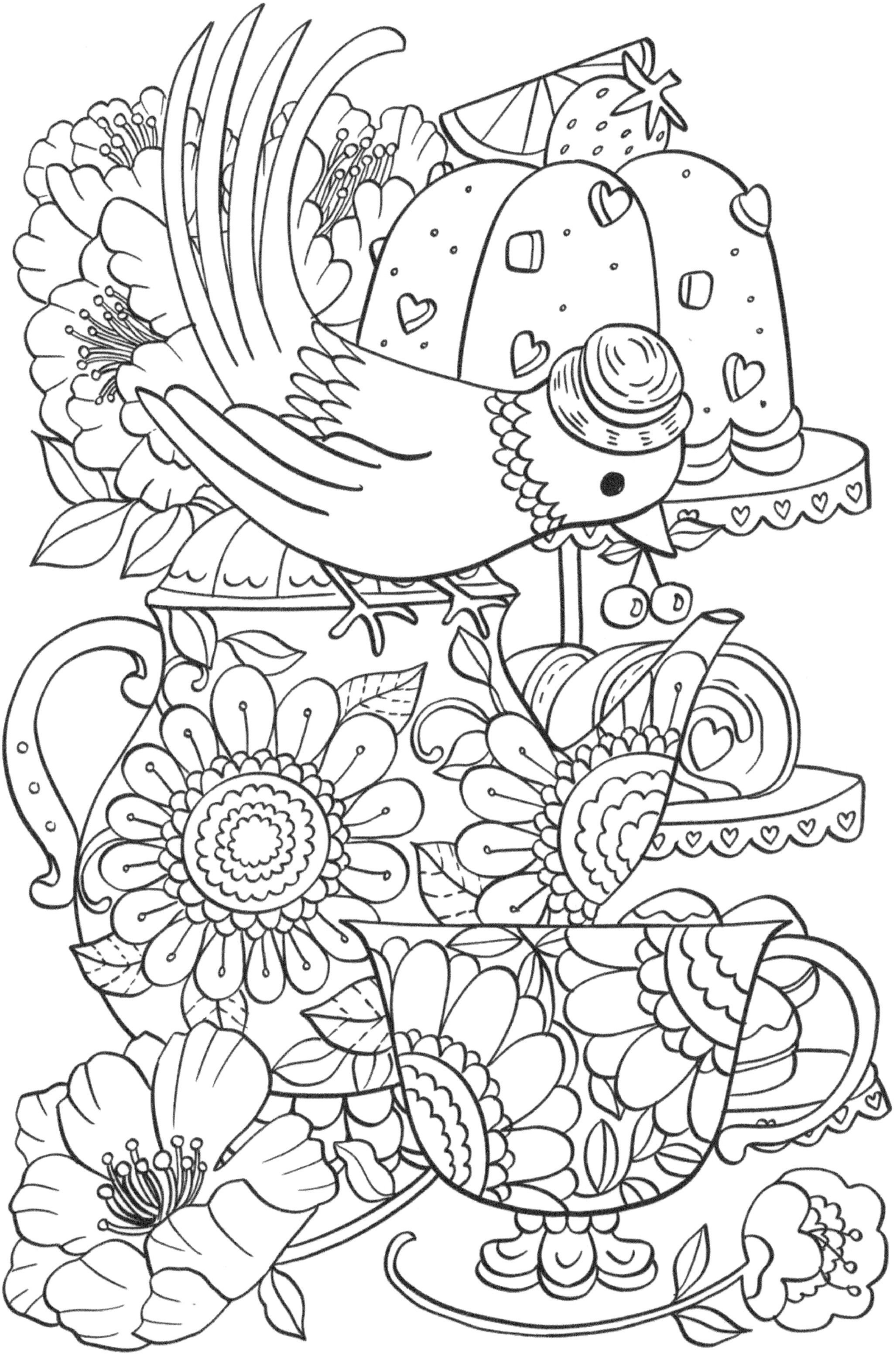

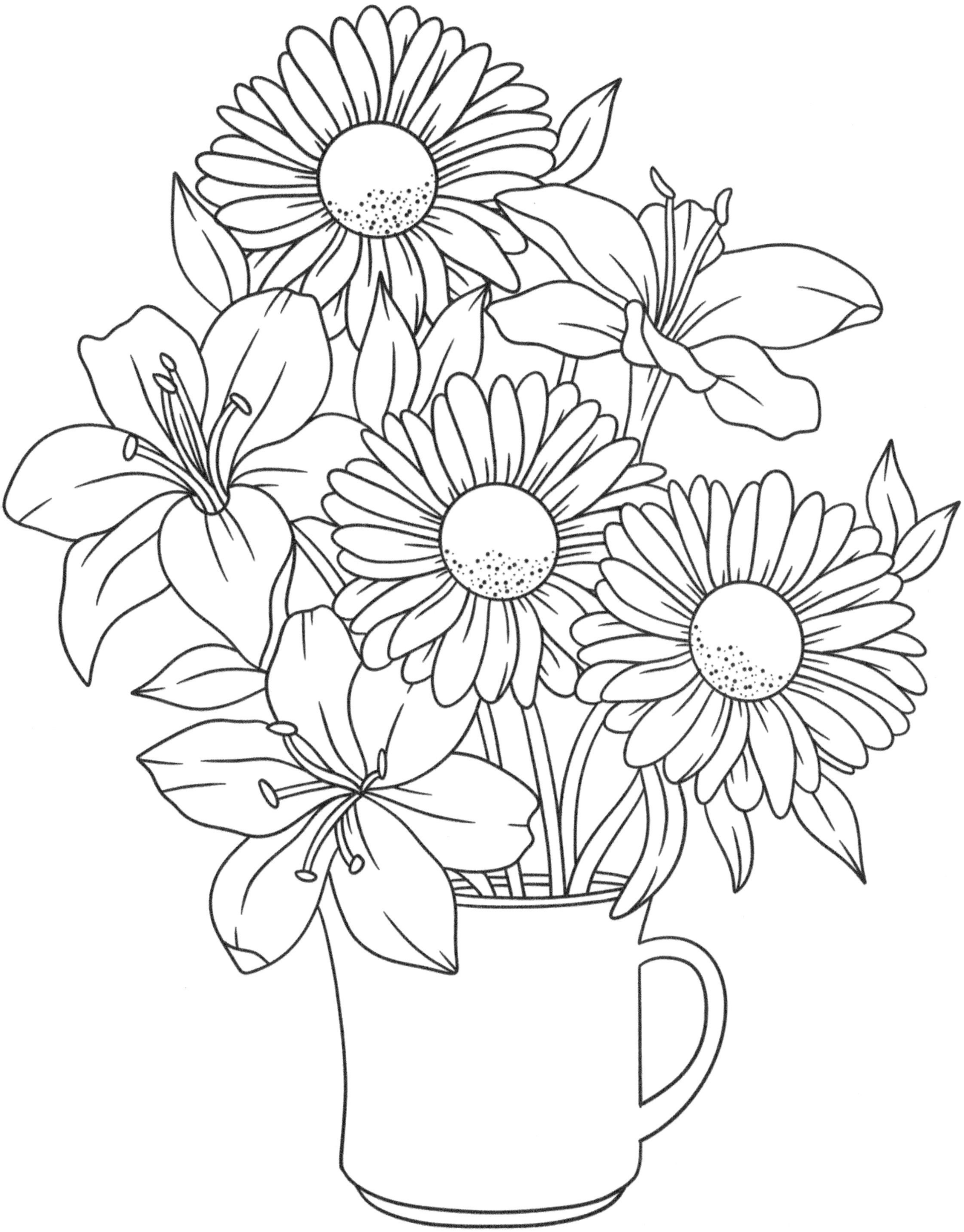

Thank You

Printed in Great Britain
by Amazon

47327615R00059